# YOUR NEW
# BABY

D1390671

# YOUR NEW BABY

PENGUIN BOOKS

Penguin
Penguin Books Australia Ltd
487 Maroondah Highway, PO Box 257
Ringwood, Victoria 3134, Australia
Penguin Books Ltd
Harmondsworth, Middlesex, England
Viking Penguin, A Division of Penguin Books USA Inc.
375 Hudson Street, New York, New York 10014, USA
Penguin Books Canada Limited
2801 John Street, Markham, Ontario, Canada L3R 1B4
Penguin Books (N.Z.) Ltd
182–190 Wairau Road, Auckland 10, New Zealand

10 9 8 7 6 5 4 3 2

Produced by Viking O'Neil
56 Claremont Street, South Yarra, Victoria 3141, Australia
A Division of Penguin Books Australia Ltd

Designed by Lynn Twelftree
Typeset in Malaysia by Typeset Gallery Sdn. Bhd.
Printed in Malaysia by Longman Malaysia Sdn. Bhd. (CLP)

National Library of Australia
Cataloguing-in-Publication data

Your new baby.

    ISBN 0 14 012946 4.

    1. Pregnancy – Australia. 2. Childbirth –
    Australia. 3. Infants – Care – Australia.
    (Series: Penguin pocket series).

618.200994

This book was prepared by Janelle Ward, with additional contributions from other writers.

# CONTENTS

~~~~~~~~~~~~~~~~~~~~~~~~~~~~~~~~~~~~~~

# INTRODUCTION

Pregnancy marks the beginning of a new chapter in your life. Ahead lie good and bad times, broken nights, and frustration – but above all love.

Like parenthood itself, being pregnant is a little like a crash course in a foreign culture. There's a new language to learn, a different lifestyle to adapt to, new people to meet, and many new experiences in store. Every pregnancy, like every baby, is different. In the coming months, however, your body, thoughts and feelings will inevitably undergo great and memorable changes – some exhilarating, and some simply irritating.

While modern medical practices and technology can take away much of the pain and the hard work that were once part and parcel of having a baby, it is also up to you to learn as much as possible so that you can make informed decisions about the many choices open to you. Today there are innumerable books, videos, classes and counsellors offering guidance on preparing for the birth and for parenthood itself. You'll also inevitably be on the receiving end of good and bad stories (and advice) from those who are mothers already. For the first-time mother this barrage of information can be awesome and confusing. In addition, many books tend to assume that all women have instinctive knowledge about baby matters and offer far too little guidance about what to expect and what to do in the new situations you will undoubtedly come across.

This book sets out to fill some of the gaps, concentrating in particular on what many of the other books don't tell you: Why is being pregnant making me feel like this? How many baby clothes do I *really* need for the first few months? How can I prepare my house, and my life, for the presence of a baby? What happens when I arrive at the hospital? What can my partner expect, and how can he help?

Creating a new human being is one of the most rewarding things that we can do. *Your New Baby* offers simple, practical and reassuring guidelines for the exciting months that lie ahead.

NOTE: For simplicity's sake, the pronouns 'she' and 'her' are used throughout this book when referring to babies and to doctors. Similarly the general term 'doctor' is used when referring to the attending professional, even though yours may well be a midwife or obstetrician.

# 1 ALL ABOUT ANTENATAL CARE

Once your pregnancy has been confirmed, it's all systems go. It's time to start counting – weeks, kilos, cigarettes, alcoholic drinks, even cups of coffee.

Regular checkups with your doctor, to ensure that the pregnancy is progressing well, constitute the more structured side of antenatal care. From the earliest days, however, there are many ways in which you too can contribute to the health and safety of your baby and prepare yourself for both the birth and your new life as a parent.

## WHEN IS YOUR BABY DUE?

To work out when your baby is due (generally referred to as your estimated date of delivery or EDD), just add 40 weeks or 280 days to the first day of your last period. If you can't remember when that was, your doctor will be able to work out an approximate date from the size of the foetus. An ultrasound scan is the most reliable guide, however, and can usually establish your due date give or take three days.

The developing baby is generally referred to as an embryo for the first eight weeks of pregnancy, after which it is called a foetus.

## SOME KNOWN DANGERS

Just as oxygen and nutrients are transferred from the mother to the foetus through the placenta, harmful substances such as alcohol, nicotine and other drugs can travel the same route and potentially retard the growth of the foetus, particularly during the critical early stages when the nervous centre, organs and limbs are being formed. While you should take precautions along the lines suggested below, don't make your life a misery – a reasonable rule of thumb is 'moderation in all things'.

### Drugs

Play it safe and take none, health permitting. If you are ill, take only those drugs which have been prescribed by a doctor (and possibly even double-checked with a pharmacist or obstetrician). Don't, on the other hand, be so cautious as to be foolish, because some conditions (such as diabetes) can increase the risk of birth defects and should therefore be treated. Be as well informed as possible, and follow your doctor's advice.

### Smoking

Nicotine reduces the efficiency of the placenta and can cause small babies or obstetric complications. It is preferable not to smoke during pregnancy: if you can't give up the habit, it is advisable to at least cut down.

# Alcohol

Heavy drinking during pregnancy can cause small babies and, in extreme cases, birth defects. While there is as yet no consensus on the daily number of drinks that are safe for pregnant women, up to two drinks a day are probably acceptable. If you do drink try to make every one last longer, perhaps diluting it with water, and intersperse each with a glass of water or juice.

# Caffeine

Excessive quantities of caffeine put strain on your digestive and circulatory systems, and may lift the foetus's heart rate. Try to limit your intake of tea, coffee, cocoa and cola drinks, and consider decaffeinated coffee and herbal teas as substitutes.

# Vitamins

Excessive doses of vitamins, particularly A, B6 and D, can cause birth defects. Take only the recommended quantities, and avoid 'macro' and 'mega' doses throughout your pregnancy.

# X-rays

X-rays should be avoided during pregnancy, as they can damage the foetus. If an X-ray is necessary, it should be carried out with a lead screen protecting your abdomen.

# Rubella or German measles

Although it is a mild illness in adults, rubella can cross the placenta and cause eye, ear and heart problems in your baby. The most dangerous period for the foetus is the first three months of pregnancy. As you cannot be vaccinated against rubella once you are pregnant, it's best to find out beforehand whether you have had it (which gives you future immunity). If you are unsure, a blood test should be taken.

## At work

If you plan to continue working during your pregnancy, take a critical look at conditions in your place of employment. Consider any possible effects of your working environment (such as chemicals or gases) on the foetus. If you are in a potentially dangerous area or position, seek a transfer for the duration of your pregnancy, either by direct approaches to your employer or through your union. If you are unsure whether there are risks, ask your doctor for advice.

Also consider factors such as the position – sitting, standing or reaching – in which you do the bulk of your work, and alter any factors necessary to improve your posture and comfort. The stress level of your job should be considered too, as stress can reduce the supply of blood (and hence oxygen and nutrients) to the foetus. Chronic stress results in increased tension in the uterine wall, and can increase the chance of miscarriage. The amount of travelling required each day may also affect the length of time you can comfortably stay at work.

## ENTER THE PROFESSIONALS

Your finances will generally dictate whether you use the public-hospital system or a private GP, obstetrician or midwife.

Personality, and attitudes to childbirth, come into it too: it is vital that you have confidence in the professional who will attend your birth, so it is worth shopping around if you have a choice.

## Family doctor, obstetrician or midwife?

If you have a family doctor you are happy with and who is qualified in obstetrics, you have an ideal base for extending the relationship. If you opt for an obstetrician or a midwife, be guided by your family doctor or by friends or acquaintances who can make a recommendation. Other factors to be considered are the location of her practice (convenient or not?), which hospitals she attends, and who would deliver your baby if she is unavailable.

An obstetrician is a doctor with six to seven years of postgraduate training in antenatal-postnatal care and childbirth. A midwife is a registered nurse who has specialised in antenatal-postnatal care and childbirth. In some Australian states midwives may take charge of low-risk deliveries but in Victoria, for example, a doctor is also required to attend.

## YOUR REGULAR CHECKUPS

You should have your first antenatal checkup within 12 weeks of becoming pregnant, but organise a referral from your GP and make an appointment as early as possible. During your pregnancy you will probably see your doctor once a month up to 28 weeks, every two weeks up to 36 weeks, and thereafter once a week until the baby is born.

Although sometimes inconvenient, these visits usually provide welcome signposts of your baby's progress and the opportunity to accustom yourself to the world of mothers and babies. Be prepared for occasional delays in the waiting room.

## Things to be discussed

At your first visit, you should arrange your booking at the place where the baby is to be born (see chapter 3). You will also be asked for all relevant details of your medical history and family tree. Do wrack your brain on this one and leave nothing out, no matter how personal or embarrassing, as such information could help to circumvent any problems during your pregnancy. If your grandmother had three miscarriages in six pregnancies, say so. If you've had a venereal disease, say so. If you were once an alcoholic, say so.

You should also discuss whether you want an ultrasound scan, or whether diagnostic tests such as amniocentesis or chorionic villus sampling are advisable (see Non-routine Tests below). Ask your doctor to explain the pros and cons of any non-routine tests.

Throughout your pregnancy, even if you do not have a choice of doctor or are visiting a hospital clinic, do ask about anything that worries you or that you don't understand. It's your pregnancy, and the doctor is there to help and advise you. Ask as many questions as you want, however petty they might seem, and don't be put off by seemingly hurried answers.

You should also ask your doctor for her views about birth options and procedures – from pain relief to circumcision – and outline your own views and wishes (see also chapter 3). Today there is some concern that non-routine procedures such as episiotomies and even caesarean operations are being performed unnecessarily. While these techniques of course have their place in the event of complications, you should know your doctor's policy on such matters.

## TESTS, TAPS AND PROBES

Pregnancy, it has often been said, is a testing time. At your first visit to the doctor – it's usually a longish one – a blood sample will be taken to find out your blood group and rhesus factor, and to check for venereal disease, rubella antibodies and anaemia. At this and every visit you will undergo a series of standard checks, including:

■ **a urine test**, to monitor the presence of sugar, protein, ketones and any urinary tract infection. Take your own urine sample, collected midstream from the first visit in the morning; a small sample, the equivalent of two or three tablespoons, is quite adequate.

■ **a weight check**, to see that your weight gain is within normal limits (see also chapter 2).

■ **a blood-pressure check**, to make sure that your blood-pressure level is within acceptable limits. High blood pressure accompanied by swelling of the hands and feet can indicate pregnancy-induced hypertension (also known as pre-eclamptic toxaemia, or toxaemia), which can reduce the efficiency of the placenta.

■ **a vaginal examination**, to ascertain the size of the foetus and its position. The doctor will insert two fingers into your vagina and press on your abdomen to palpate the uterus. She may also insert a speculum to inspect your cervix and take a cervical (or 'pap') smear. Towards the end of your pregnancy, by palpating your uterus your doctor can ascertain whether the baby's head is engaged in the pelvic cavity ready for the birth. At this stage she may also check the size of your pelvis, which needs to be large enough for the baby's head to pass through.

■ **a breast examination**, to identify any problems such as inverted nipples.

## Non-routine tests

There are a number of other tests you may undergo during your pregnancy. While you should be guided by your doctor's advice, ask her to explain the reasons for any non-routine test and any possible risks attached.

If diagnostic tests such as chorionic villus sampling or amniocentesis indicate that chromosomal defects are present in the foetus, you have the choice of aborting the pregnancy. It is advisable to discuss such a possibility with your partner and make your decision before the test.

Some of the more common non-routine tests available during pregnancy are outlined below.

■ **ultrasound** (any time). Using high-frequency sound waves, an ultrasound scan provides a clear picture of the foetus. It is used to determine your due date or to chart your baby's progress; it may also be used, rather like a microscope, during other diagnostic tests such as amniocentesis. The procedure is quite painless, although you are required to have a relatively full bladder and this can be uncomfortable. Depending on the position of the foetus, it is possible to ascertain its sex, if you want to know – if you don't, be sure to tell the doctor beforehand. Ultrasound is generally regarded as safe, although the British government has recommended that it not be undertaken routinely or regularly during pregnancy.

■ **amniocentesis** (14–16 weeks) This procedure, in which fluid is removed from the amniotic sac, is used to identify any chromosomal abnormalities (such as Down's syndrome) in the foetus. Until recently it was generally performed only on women over 37 or with a known risk of birth defects, but it is now thought that other factors may be more relevant than age. Using ultrasound for guidance, a needle is inserted through your abdomen to extract a sample of amniotic fluid for analysis. The test is uncomfortable rather than painful, but can be distressing to anticipate. There is a small risk of miscarriage.

- **chorionic villus sampling** (c. 10 weeks). This test, which is beginning to replace amniocentesis, also determines chromosomal abnormalities and certain other hereditary conditions in the foetus. It is similar to a cervical smear but is performed under ultrasound: some of the placental tissue is removed with a catheter, and then analysed. There is a slight risk of miscarriage.
- **glucose tolerance test** (c. 24 weeks) This test, which is increasingly a routine procedure, is used to detect diabetes in the mother-to-be. You are given a small quantity of glucose to drink and about an hour later a blood sample is taken via a prick in the fingertip. If the reading is above a specified level you will undergo a more comprehensive test, which takes about three hours.
- **foetal heart monitoring** (c. 35 weeks onwards). Checking the heartbeat of the foetus is a useful means of verifying its wellbeing, and this procedure may be used if there is any cause for concern. An ultrasound disc, attached to a nearby monitor, is strapped to your abdomen and the foetal heartbeat is both charted on tickertape and magnified through a loudspeaker.

## But I'm so healthy!

If you are having an easy pregnancy and look and feel healthy, you may wonder why it is necessary to see your doctor so frequently and to undergo so many tests. It's all about being better safe than sorry: the routine and not-so-routine checks are designed to alert the doctor to any condition that is potentially dangerous for either you or your baby. Even your general manner and appearance allow her to assess your well-being and help you through any problems.

## ANTENATAL CLASSES

Antenatal classes are designed to help you become more in tune with the changes your body undergoes during pregnancy, and with what you should be doing in preparation for the birth. Such classes are of great benefit even if you are doing your own preparatory reading, as the contact with other pregnant women and their partners can be both beneficial and reassuring. Classes are offered by most hospitals, some health clubs, some infant-welfare centres, and independent organisations. Ask your doctor or hospital for further information.

Anyone who intends to be at the birth of your baby (particularly your partner) is generally encouraged to attend the classes with you. There is usually some useful information about what your partner may expect during both your pregnancy and the birth, and how he can help.

Some institutions offer classes relatively late in pregnancy. If you can it's worthwhile attending before the halfway mark, to give you time to practise your exercises and to digest and make use of the knowledge gained, all of which will give you greater confidence in achieving the type of birth you want. Some courses offer several classes earlier in the pregnancy and sessions in the last few months, which is a good compromise given a pregnant woman's capacity for forgetfulness.

## The childbirth educator

This position is filled informally by a variety of professionals –
midwives, physiotherapists, social workers, health-care workers,
and teachers who are also mothers – who have undertaken
special training in the field of childbirth education. There will
be at least one such person at your antenatal classes; in certain
circumstances, she may be available to attend the birth.

# 2 YOUR CHANGING BODY

Perhaps the earliest sign that you're pregnant will be tender breasts and slightly enlarged nipples; there may also be some nausea or uncharacteristic tiredness – or none of these symptoms.

Every pregnancy is different. Some women feel sensational, sexy and superfit; others feel frumpy, fatigued and fearful. Whatever the case, your body is destined to undergo many dramatic changes as the hormones associated with pregnancy (especially the sex hormones oestrogen and progesterone) take over. It is a great help to understand what is happening and why, so prepare yourself by reading and learning about the likely physical and mental changes in store. As well as looking after yourself and the growing baby by eating carefully, it is worth pampering yourself a little to help you look and feel your best.

## WEIGHT GAIN

The 'normal' weight gain during pregnancy is between 10 kilograms and 13 kilograms, most of it occurring during the second half of the pregnancy. The gain is caused by the growth of the baby (an average of 3.5 kilograms at birth), the placenta and amniotic fluid, your enlarged uterus and breasts, an increase in your blood volume and body fluid, and the storage of reserve fat and protein. You may look very pregnant at eight weeks or decidedly unpregnant at 18 weeks. There is usually some thickening of the waist by 10 to 14 weeks, but don't count on it.

Your weight will be checked at each antenatal visit. If you feel good and your doctor is happy with your progress, don't worry too much about your weight and try not to make comparisons with others. Don't be alarmed if the gain is above average for one or two months, or if it is static for a similar period – the chances are that if you are being sensible, it will average out. Do remember, though, that large amounts of extra fat may be difficult to shed after the baby is born. In addition, an above-average weight gain in the last 20 weeks may indicate excess fat or fluid retention, which in association with high blood pressure can be a sign of pregnancy-induced hypertension.

## DIET

If your diet and dietary knowledge are poor, you now have a great incentive to improve them. The old 'eating for two' catchcry does not mean that you should double your food intake during pregnancy; it is true, however, that you're now providing for a developing baby who is a demanding dinner guest. The foetus has the first serve of oxygen and nutrients from your blood, so both of you may suffer if your diet is poor.

The uterus is a veritable powerhouse of activity as the foetus develops, and thus demands a good supply of fuel. Not just any fuel will do, however: you need more of certain nutrients – particularly calcium, phosphorous, iron and folic acid – but no extra fat or sugar. Basically, you should eat from each of the following four categories every day: dairy products; meat and fish (or peas, beans, nuts and seeds if you're a vegetarian) and eggs; fruit and vegetables; cereals, grains and breads. Also review the way in which foods are prepared or cooked: try non-oily dressings with your salads, and grill rather than fry your meats. Ask your doctor for advice or printed guidelines.

In short, be sensible: pregnancy is not a time for overeating, but nor is it a time for dieting. Eating well will help you look and feel better, and may help you avoid some of pregnancy's less pleasant side-effects, such as constipation.

## Nausea and indigestion

If you suffer from nausea, you may prefer to eat a series of nutritious snacks rather than three meals a day. Avoid fats and fatty foods.

As your pregnancy advances, main meals may leave you feeling overfull and prone to indigestion or heartburn. Try eating smaller, frequent meals and in particular avoid a heavy meal in the evening – it's no fun eating at 8 p.m. and going to bed two hours later with a quarter of a kilo of meat sitting just under your ribcage.

# EXERCISE

Pregnancy is not the time to run a marathon if you have never run 100 metres before. On the other hand, nor is it the time put your sporting gear in mothballs and take up crosswords. A reasonable standard of fitness will stand you and the baby in good stead – helping you to relax and improving your oxygen intake and blood circulation.

Generally, you should keep on with any sport or exercise you enjoy until it becomes too tiring or you feel too uncomfortable. Check with your doctor if you have any doubts or queries, and do listen to your body: if you come off the squash court with an aching pelvis or with back pain, either modify your play or take up a less demanding sport. Swimming is generally considered to be the best all-round exercise and it gives you a welcome sense of weightlessness, particularly when your body becomes unwieldy in the later months. Like yoga, it is also a very relaxing form of exercise.

## Specific exercises

There are many exercises designed specifically for pregnancy and childbirth. They help minimise side-effects such as backache, give you greater awareness of and control over your body, and help prepare your muscles (particularly those of the abdomen, back and legs) for the demands of giving birth. You will be introduced to such exercises at antenatal classes, and special exercise classes are organised by maternal and child health centres. Ask your doctor for information.

It is particularly important to exercise your pelvic floor muscles (those supporting the lower pelvic organs), which are weakened by the hormonal and weight changes of pregnancy. Strengthening them will improve your ability to relax the pelvic area and push out your baby, improve the elasticity of your perineum (the area between the vagina and the anus) for the birth, and help you regain better control over your bladder after the baby is born. The exercise is like trying to stop yourself urinating: tighten the muscles around your vagina and anus, hold for 10 seconds, then relax. Repeat this exercise as often as possible throughout the day, and during sexual intercourse.

## MATERNITY CLOTHES

What you wear during your pregnancy will depend on your personal style and, of course, your wallet. Some women proudly adopt the maternity look almost as soon as their pregnancy is confirmed. Others prefer to dress in a low-key manner throughout.

Even at about four months, you may get away with holding together the waist of your trousers or skirts with safety pins. As your waist inevitably thickens and your breasts get larger, it's time to think big or at least bigger. You might opt for regular maternity clothes with tent shapes or gusset and drawstring waists. Alternatively, you might simply wear outsized versions of your usual clothes.

Whatever the case, make sure that whatever you buy or borrow is comfortable when you sit. It is unwise to wear anything that might restrict your blood flow, and something that looks and feels good when you stand can be a devil in disguise when you collapse into a chair or get behind the wheel of a car.

Maternity boutiques can be expensive, so investigate warehouses and recycle shops. Don't go overboard – you will only need very large clothes for about the last two months, and you probably won't want to see your pregnancy clothes for quite a while after the birth. There are several details to remember, however.

- If you wear a bra, it should be well-fitting and comfortable. For most of your pregnancy any unwired bra will do, but do have it fitted by a trained assistant. If you intend to breast-feed, invest in two to three nursing bras in the last weeks of your pregnancy, by which stage the assistant should be able to estimate how much bigger your breasts will become when they're filled with milk.

- If you wear stockings or tights, buy those labelled 'support' or 'maternity' as they are designed to give stretchy support and are much more comfortable in advanced pregnancy.

- Well-fitting and comfortable shoes, preferably with flat or low heels, will help to prevent backache. Avoid constricting straps, as your feet can swell remarkably if you have any fluid build-up, especially if you're on your feet for extended periods.

- If you normally wear bikini-style pants, keep on doing so as you'll find that they sit neatly and comfortably under the bulge.
- One good outfit is a must for the ego, if you can afford it. When you're feeling and looking big, it's a boost to have something special to wear.

## YOUR BREASTS

During pregnancy your breasts and nipples will become bigger and more tender. Some women find that they become sore, others that they are simply more sensitive. Your nipples will also become darker, and the breast veins will be more noticeable. Late in the pregnancy, gentle massaging of the breast around the nipple may produce a yellowish fluid called colostrum, which provides all the baby's food requirements for the two to three days before you start producing milk. (Don't worry if you try but can't produce colostrum, however, as it is not noticeable to many women until after the birth.) Even if you don't usually wear a bra, you will probably feel more comfortable with one as your breasts become larger and heavier. There is some evidence to suggest that they do little to stop breasts sagging, however, and are therefore not essential. If you choose to wear a bra, get a good one and get it properly fitted, making sure that it is comfortable.

Pregnant women were once told to regularly draw out their nipples, rub in cream, and even sunbathe topless to toughen their breasts for the rigours of breastfeeding, but such preparation is now generally considered unnecessary.

## YOUR SKIN, HAIR AND NAILS

The high levels of hormones in your body during pregnancy may affect you in less expected ways.

In some women the facial skin darkens temporarily (sometimes in patches), which can be disguised with foundation cream. Your skin will return to normal after the birth, so don't attempt to cure the problem with chemicals. Your skin texture may also change – you may have the clearest complexion you've ever had, you may get pimples for the first time in your life, or you may find you're allergic to cosmetics you've used for years. If problems do occur, ask your pharmacist or doctor for advice.

Your hair may also undergo some changes, the most common of which are increased oiliness and a thicker head of hair (the latter being due to reduced hair loss). You may also notice a slight increase in, and darkening of, the hair on your face and body: as with skin changes, this should disappear after the baby is born, so don't do anything drastic. Due to the unpredictable effects of the pregnancy hormones, it is advisable not to have your hair permed or coloured while you're pregnant.

Among the benefits of pregnancy is the likelihood that your nails will strengthen and look better than ever. If, on the other hand, they develop a tendency to split or break, use a nail strengthening product and consider increasing your calcium intake.

## Pregnancy cosmetics

In addition to vitamin and mineral supplements, you will probably be tempted to add a few specialist creams, lotions and potions to the shelves. If you are experiencing skin-tone changes and allergic reactions, it may well be worth investigating non-perfumed cosmetics. Don't, however, be talked into buying an expensive wonder product 'guaranteed' to prevent stretchmarks or cure your skin problems, as such recommendations seem to alter every year. Most women are predisposed to certain changes, and it's most likely that you'll return to normal after the birth. A balanced diet is your best weapon.

## YOUR MENTAL WELLBEING

It has been commented that pregnancy is one long party for your hormones, and your body is the venue. The resulting physical and mental changes affect every woman differently. You may feel exhilarated or miserable, enthusiastic or full of apprehension: most women experience all these feelings at some time during the 40 weeks of pregnancy, and some feel them all at the same time. It may be cold comfort, but feelings such as depression, irritability, forgetfulness and placidity, emotional fragility, and violent mood swings are common side-effects of pregnancy. You may also experience unexpected doubts and fears. The answer is to unload your worries to a sympathetic partner, a mother (either your own or a friend who's just been through it all), or your doctor.

Every prospective parent at time stage asks 'Will my baby be normal?' Do confront and discuss this fear so that you can relax and enjoy your pregnancy. If there is any basis for your fears, present the facts. Are you worried about a cousin who has some mental or physical handicap? Are you fretting about a drug you've taken or an alcoholic binge before you knew you were pregnant? Are you concerned about your age? An ultrasound, or amniocentesis if you're in a high-risk category, may set your mind at ease.

Other common fears, particularly for first–time mothers, include anxiety about labour and the birth, concern about your changing body and the effect this may have on your partner, misgivings about having to leave work, financial worries, doubts about your ability to love and look after a baby, and the potential loss of your freedom. Again, do discuss these and any other concerns with your doctor, or with someone else who knows you well and preferably understands the emotional swings of pregnancy.

## YOUR SEX LIFE

Unless you have a history of miscarriage or premature labour, sex is quite safe throughout your pregnancy. You need have no fears about dislodging, denting or infecting the foetus, or instigating premature labour. You and your partner will probably notice extra vaginal secretions, which are quite normal.

Some studies suggest that orgasm in the last weeks of pregnancy may help to soften the cervix in preparation for labour.

Your appetite for sex may alter or fluctuate. You may feel quite uninterested, particularly if you are tired or nauseous, or your desire may be greater than usual, particularly if your body is generally more sensitive. It is important for you and your partner to discuss your feelings, and for neither to feel rejected.

As your bulk increases later in the pregnancy, you may need to try different positions during intercourse. You should also consider alternative forms of intimacy, such as just kissing and cuddling, orgasm without intercourse, or oral sex. If sex is uncomfortable, discuss the problems with your doctor.

## COMMON SIDE-EFFECTS OF PREGNANCY

During pregnancy you can expect many changes to your body and any number of minor discomforts. Below is a checklist of some of the most common disorders, and ways in which you can help to minimise them. If you suffer from some or even all of the following complaints, take comfort in the thought that you're not alone. You may also be cheered by the thought that it's not all in vain – there is a baby at the end of it all – and that your next pregnancy may be a breeze...

### Backache and pelvic pain

This can affect all pregnant women, particularly in the later months as your ligaments soften in readiness for the birth. It is often worse for those who have already had a child, have poor posture, or stand for long periods. The extra weight you're carrying in front will inevitably put added strain on your back, so take a closer look at your posture and even the way you bend and lift. Wear low-heeled shoes whenever possible, check your posture several times a day, and stand tall. Exercise to strengthen your back and improve its muscle tone, and avoid lifting heavy weights. Also check your sleeping position: avoid sleeping on your back in the later months, and try placing a board under the mattress.

Severe, rhythmic back pain should be reported to your doctor or midwife, as it could indicate a threatened miscarriage or the start of labour.

## Bleeding
Any vaginal bleeding during pregnancy should be reported to your doctor or midwife immediately. Light spotting is not unusual in the first few weeks, but continued bleeding (particularly if it is accompanied by pain) may indicate a threatened miscarriage.

## Breathlessness
About 75 per cent of pregnant women experience some breathlessness, particularly after strenuous activity. It can be alarming, but will not affect your baby: it is caused the decreasing space available for your lungs to expand as the uterus enlarges. Rest for a few minutes if and when it occurs.

## Constipation

Constipation is another common discomfort of the later months of pregnancy, caused mainly by the relaxing of the intestine wall so that food moves through the bowel more slowly. It can be exacerbated by iron and folic acid supplements. Drink more fluids, eat more roughage, and try to take more exercise. If all else fails, try a mild natural (senna) laxative.

## Cramps

Foot or leg cramps are often experienced at night, particularly in later pregnancy. In the event of an attack, press your leg flat to the bed and have your partner push your foot back towards your body. As preventive measures, increase your fluid intake and try sleeping with your feet raised higher than your head. In severe cases, additional doses of vitamin B and calcium may be prescribed.

## Dizziness or fainting

Dizzy spells are a by-product of changes to your circulatory system. They are usually caused by a sudden fall in blood pressure, and are most likely to occur when you stand up too quickly or stand for prolonged periods. Frequent attacks, particularly if associated with pain or vaginal bleeding, should be reported to your doctor immediately.

## False or Braxton Hicks contractions

These painless and irregular contractions of the uterus can occur throughout the pregnancy, but are more common (and noticeable) towards the end. They are in fact the uterus practising for real labour; as long as the contractions are irregular, there is no need for concern.

## Food cravings

Thought to be caused by hormonal activity, these can occur at any time. The items in demand vary enormously between women and between pregnancies, but are often in the carbohydrate or fruit categories. Don't be concerned as long as the cravings don't become too bizarre – if they do, notify your doctor.

## Frequent urination

The need to urinate tends to become more frequent as pressure is exerted on the bladder, at first by the enlarging uterus and later by the baby's head. This may mean several visits to the loo during the night, which some say is nature's way of preparing us for broken sleep after the birth! There's nothing you can do to help, except to empty your bladder yet again and avoid long periods standing.

## Haemorrhoids

Again a side-effect of the later months, haemorrhoids are inflamed veins that appear around the anus. They are caused by straining to empty the bowels when constipated, or by excessive pressure on the blood vessels (such as when the baby's head is engaged in the pelvis). Keep your fibre intake high to avoid constipation. Ice packs can help reduce swelling, and special ointments and suppositories are available.

## Heartburn

Indigestion or heartburn is particularly common in the later months, and is usually worse when you're lying down. It is caused by the enlarging uterus pushing up against the stomach and the acid contents of the stomach returning into the oesophagus. Eat smaller and lighter meals, particularly in the evening, and sleep propped up on extra pillows. Ask your doctor to recommend a mild antacid, or try some of the herbal teas that are readily available.

## Incontinence

In the later months you may involuntarily pass a few drops of urine when you laugh, cough or sneeze. This is caused by pressure on the bladder and the relaxing of your intestinal muscles in preparation for the birth. The best safeguard is to practise your pelvic floor exercises. If the problem is serious, consider wearing sanitary pads.

## Itchiness

As your abdomen swells and tightens, it is quite common for it to become itchy. Severe itching all over the body should be reported to your doctor, as it may indicate some medical disorder.

## Nausea or morning sickness

About 50 per cent of pregnant women suffer from nausea during pregnancy, a reaction to the increased levels of hormones in the body. Ranging from mild nausea through to vomiting, it usually occurs in the first 12 weeks but may persist for longer and recur late in the pregnancy. While it does often attack first thing in the morning, in fact it can strike at any time of the day or night. However unappealing food may seem, don't neglect to eat and do try to have something to eat and drink before you get out of bed. Avoid aggravating foods, particularly fats, and eat smaller meals. Medication is available in severe cases.

## Nosebleeds

Nosebleeds, like bleeding from the gums, are not unusual during pregnancy and are caused by your increased blood supply – they do not mean you have high blood pressure. In the case of nosebleeds, an ice pack may help; for bleeding gums, try a saltwater mouth wash.

## Sleep problems

You may find sleeping difficult at any time during your pregnancy, although it is more common in the later months. The reasons may be physical: needing to urinate, cramps, indigestion, or simply the baby moving about. On the other hand they may be psychological: anxiety, excitement or fear. Discuss the problem with your doctor and mention any specific worries that are keeping you awake. A warm drink may help, and a mild sleeping pill may be prescribed if your daytime activities are suffering as a result.

## Stretchmarks

These lines, which fade from purplish–red to silvery-white, may appear on the breasts, upper legs and arms, bottom and abdomen. Some women are predisposed to stretchmarks, but they may also occur in the event of excessive weight gain. Creams and oils are of dubious value, but they will help condition your skin: if they give you hope, spread them on.

## Swollen feet, ankles and fingers

This is generally caused by oedema (the retention of extra fluid in your body) and by the extra weight you're carrying. It is likely to be exacerbated by hot weather or by standing a lot. Try to find time to rest with your feet up, and remove any restricting items such as finger rings or shoes with tight straps.

Swelling which persists or which occurs elsewhere on your body could indicate pregnancy-induced hypertension, so notify your doctor.

## Tiredness

Fatigue or sleepiness during pregnancy, particularly in the first three months, is not surprising – your body is doing a lot of extra work. It may be frustrating if you're used to being active, but it is a warning to slow down. If you can't manage extra

sleep, at least try to get some rest and whenever possible sit
with your feet up.

## Vaginal changes

Your vagina will change colour (usually darkening) during pregnancy because of your changing blood circulation. Increased
vaginal discharge is normal throughout pregnancy, but may
become more noticeable in the later months. If the discharge is
discoloured or smelly and accompanied by itching, notify your
doctor as it could indicate an infection such as thrush.

## Varicose and spider veins

Varicose veins are caused by increased pressure on your legs.
They tend to be hereditary and can appear at any time, but are
more likely to occur in the later months of pregnancy. Try to
avoid excessive weight gain, keep your feet up as much as
possible, and consider wearing support tights or stockings. In
many cases they will disappear after the pregnancy, and those
that do remain can be surgically removed.

Networks of fine blue or red 'spider' veins are also common,
particularly around the ankles, and are generally caused by the
extra weight you're carrying. They too should disappear after
the baby is born.

## GREAT MOMENTS

Happily, pregnancy affords some unparalleled excitements
which undoubtedly help compensate for its discomforts and
inconveniences. Even if you're an unwilling or unbelieving

parent-to-be, it's unforgettable when you get the first physical proofs that it's really a little human being that you're carrying.

## First flutters

You are likely to feel your first flutter from the growing baby anywhere between 16 and 22 weeks, although often later. It may feel like wind, but is somehow different. This is usually a magic moment: it's communication, and concrete evidence that there is something in there and it's alive and moving about. No matter how definite or prolonged that initial activity, however, you can be sure that as soon as you encourage someone to feel the movement all action will stop.

## Kicks, bumps and hiccups

The first tiny flutters very quickly become more forceful, and last longer. As your pregnancy advances, the foetus may kick, squirm and roll with such force that your abdomen becomes quite distorted. By noting when each burst of activity occurs, you may be able to work out the foetus's sleeping and wakeful times. Be prepared, too, for foetal hiccup attacks, which will undoubtedly worry you more they trouble the baby.

## Ultrasound – your first baby snap

While ultrasound is used principally for clinical purposes (see chapter 1), at the end of the session you will be given a small photo rather like a Polaroid snap. At 16 weeks, about the time when an ultrasound is commonly performed, the foetus is about 18 centimetres long and completely formed, though with a large head. The image will be a little fuzzy, but with the doctor's direction you may be able to see the entire head and body, moving limbs, and the heartbeat. The photo you take home with you will give you much enjoyment as well as reassurance.

Your partner and any other family members are generally welcome at the scan. Do encourage your partner to attend, as most men who have done so find it an unexpectedly moving experience, as the first concrete evidence of the baby's humanity.

## Boy or girl?

Today you can find out the sex of your baby long before the birth. This is a personal decision for you and your partner. Some couples opt to find out in advance because it gives them a stronger sense of the baby's identity (particularly in the case of the father, who doesn't have much else to go on), or simply so that they can decide on and start using a name or choose a nursery colour scheme. Others – and probably the majority – prefer to leave themselves with a surprise at the end of the day.

## The foetal heartbeat

The procedure of foetal heart monitoring (see chapter 1) gives you an amplified sound of the baby's heart as early as 12 weeks and certainly by 16 weeks. The rapid thump-thump (120–160 beats a minute) can be startling at first, but like ultrasound provides reassuring proof of the baby's vitality.

# 3 CHOICES AND DECISIONS

There are a number of matters you should investigate as early as possible in your pregnancy. You will, for example, need to sort out your practical affairs. What medical and hospital costs are involved in antenatal care and the birth itself? If you're working, are you eligible for maternity leave or your partner for paternity leave? There's also a surprising amount of decision-making to do. Who's going to deliver your baby and where? What sort of birth do you want? Who do you intend to have there for support? Will you breast- or bottle-feed?

Below is a checklist of the practical matters you should consider now. Chapter 9 looks in more detail at the issues involved in child care.

## HEALTH INSURANCE

Check your health cover, if you have any. If you want your baby delivered by the doctor of your choice in a private hospital with a private room, without having to part with thousands of dollars, you should have intermediate or top hospital cover; consider additional cover for extras such as the use of an anaesthetist. With this cover you should then have to pay only for certain pharmaceuticals and your telephone calls. The bad news is that if you are already pregnant and have no health insurance, it's too late as there is a nine-months qualifying period.

Medicare will cover most costs in a public hospital. It is likely that you will be seen by different doctors during your antenatal visits, however, and you cannot choose the doctor who delivers your baby as you will be assisted by whomever is on duty at the time.

## Home births

Different health funds have slightly different policies on home births, but a small refund is generally available for the cost of the birth and any postnatal visits by domiciliary nurses. Medicare covers home births attended by a doctor, but not those at which a midwife assists. If you are planning a home birth, consider ambulance cover in case of an emergency.

# WORK ARRANGEMENTS

## Maternity and paternity leave

If you're working, check with your employer or your union whether you're entitled to maternity leave. You may be entitled to paid or unpaid leave, even if your position is only part-time. If not, your employer may agree to hold your job for you for a set period.

Some organisations also provide paternity leave, with or without pay, so get your partner to investigate the situation at his place of work.

## Returning to work after the birth

If you intend to return to the workforce after the baby has arrived, discuss the possibilities and the problems well in advance. Try to leave yourself some flexibility, however, as after the baby is born your needs and priorities may change. Ask about part-time work, or the possibility of working from home. Also find out about any work-based child-care options.

## CHILD CARE

Surprising at it may seem, particularly to first-time mothers, you should inquire about child-care options as early as possible in your pregnancy. This applies not only if you're planning an early return to work, but also if you think you might like a regular day off. Your options are informal care (family or friends), government or private day-care centres, or family day care. Inquire at your local council about arrangements and centres in your area, bearing in mind that many child-care centres have very long waiting lists, particularly for the 0–2 age group.

## WHAT TYPE OF BIRTH?

Today there is increasing emphasis on natural births, with a minimum of technical intervention. While circumstances may dictate a certain course when the times comes, and when it starts to hurt you may not even care, it is sensible to investigate the various approaches available so that you can discuss their pros and cons with your doctor. The type of birth you would like may also influence your choice of hospital.

## Approaches to natural childbirth

Perhaps the most publicised approach to natural childbirth is the Leboyer method, which was devised by a French obstetrician. It seeks to remove some of the trauma of the birth through a gentler transition for the baby from the uterus to the world. Its main features are delivery in a quiet and dimly lit environment, the baby being placed immediately on the mother's abdomen (which also allows any mucus in the lungs to drain naturally without the need for suctioning), and the umbilical cord not being clamped immediately (so that baby can settle into a normal breathing pattern at its own pace). The newborn is immersed in a deep warm bath to simulate the environment of the uterus, and any tests made on the baby should, if possible, be done within the mother's reach. Many hospitals offer at least a modified version of the Leboyer birth – dim lighting, a minimum of noise, the baby being placed on the mother's stomach, and a warm bath being given by the father and/or mother.

Other approaches include the Odent birth, which also advocates a minimum of light, noise and technological intervention. It recommends that the delivery room be as non-clinical as possible and ideally contain only a cushioned platform, a birthing chair and a stereo. The mother should be allowed to be spontaneous and uninhibited during the birth, and be encouraged to adopt whatever position she chooses during labour and the birth itself. This type of birth is best achieved at home or in a birthing centre, although some hospitals also now encourage a similarly unfettered approach.

The Lamaze method involves both physical and psychological preparation for childbirth. As with psychoprophylaxis (see Pain Relief below), the aim is to control or at least reduce pain through education, breathing and relaxation. This approach requires strong links between you and your partner, who should train with you, and also between you and your doctor.

Water births, which take place in a large tub or even a swimming pool, are also intended to make the baby's transition from the uterus as painless as possible, and the birth as relaxing as possible for both mother and baby. A skilled midwife or doctor is essential. Few hospitals offer this option.

## Delivery positions

The longstanding practice of giving birth lying on your back is said to have been devised in the 18th century for the convenience of the attending doctor. It has recently lost favour, as it limits the mother's ability to play an active part in the birth, reduces the flow of blood to the baby, and can increase the likelihood of an episiotomy.

If gravity can lend a hand, why not let it? Many childbirth educators now support the age-old tradition of women remaining upright and active during labour. They suggest the mother-to-be should walk as much as possible during the first stage of labour (when the cervix is dilating), and many mothers agree that this makes labour easier. For the transition stage (when the cervix is almost fully dilated but it is not time to push), consider squatting on or beside the bed, sitting on or astride a chair, kneeling or on all fours, or lying on one side with a knee drawn up. For delivery, squatting or kneeling is thought to be the most efficient position (as long as you are comfortable and have done some practice during the pregnancy), as the pelvis is thus at its widest and gravity helps the baby's descent.

It should be noted that as yet only a small number of hospitals actively encourage you to adopt these positions.

## WHERE'S IT TO BE?

The type of birth you want may determine the venue. If you want to deliver in the bath you may have to opt for your home, whereas an Odent birth may be possible in a birthing centre. Be guided by your doctor, by the grapevine, by responses from the hospitals about their policies and procedures, and by their locations. For your own convenience and that of your potential visitors, it's advisable not to choose a hospital that is a long way from home.

If you want a particular birthing centre or hospital, book now. Birthing centres are in increasing demand but still limited in number, so there are usually long waiting lists. Some hospitals also need to be booked as early as possible to ensure a bed, let alone a private room.

# Hospitals

In making your choice of hospital, do ask lots of questions about their procedures (see also chapter 5). Can I have a Leboyer-style delivery? Can my family visit whenever they wish? Can I choose whether or not my baby rooms in? How long can I stay in hospital? Is domiciliary care available after the birth?

Even if you have no choice of hospital, ask any questions that are important to you and state your views. Also inquire about antenatal classes and a possible tour of the labour wards and maternity sections.

If it is within your means, a private room or at least a room with only one other mother is preferable. A room with four mothers (and thus four babies for much of the time) can be a very noisy place in which to to try to recuperate.

# Birthing centres

You need to be in the low-risk category for a birthing centre delivery. Such centres, which are usually attached to hospitals, are essentially a compromise between the home birth and the labour ward. Designed rather like a motel room, with a double bed and other comforts, they allow you to give birth in a non-clinical environment but with emergency back-up only a trolley ride away.

# Home births

For a home birth, your doctor should help you with the necessary preparations and modifications. It is advisable to organise some postnatal help well in advance: consider a roster of family and friends, or home help (which might be available through your local council). Regular visits from a domiciliary nurse are advisable, to make postnatal checks on you and your baby and to assist you until you are ready to cope alone.

## How long to stay in hospital

While many new mothers welcome the opportunity for a well-needed rest and a chance to learn as much as possible about caring for a baby before going it alone, others are keen to get home as soon as possible.

Discuss this matter with both your doctor and the hospital. Most hospitals encourage mother and baby to stay for up to a week after the birth. Birthing centres, on the other hand, encourage healthy and confident mothers to go home after a day or two. If you are using a birthing centre but wish to have some extra time in hospital, arrange to be transferred to a room or ward elsewhere in the hospital for a few days.

## THE LABOUR WARD AUDIENCE

You should also start thinking now about who you want at the birth.

### Your partner?

Today it is accepted practice to have your partner in attendance, but make sure that you do really want him present and that he wants to be there. Discuss any misgivings that either of you may have, and also talk about the experience with any of your friends who have been through it already. Most fathers who have witnessed the birth of their child agree that it is an immensely exciting and rewarding experience. On a more practical level, the presence of your partner can ensure that you have company throughout the labour, in the event of the nursing staff being needed elsewhere from time to time. The other side of the coin is that the presence of a domineering, unwilling or squeamish partner may be a hindrance rather than a help.

A small number of fathers are now cutting the umbilical cord and even delivering the baby. Would you like him to do this? Does he want to do it? Will the hospital allow it?

## Family and friends?

Consider whether you'd like any other family members to attend the birth. Check your hospital's policy and ask for their opinions and advice. In the case of children, they should be fully prepared beforehand and there should be someone available to look after and reassure them. Do consider the possible effect on them of seeing you in pain.

## Which professionals?

Do you want to engage a paediatrician for an early assessment of the baby? Some paediatricians argue that their detailed examination of a newborn can mean the difference between a normal or handicapped life. On the other hand, the attendance of a specialist is expensive; in addition, many serious problems can be diagnosed during the pregnancy, and doctors and midwives are trained to check the newborn and monitor its transition from foetus to baby.

Do you want a 'coach' to guide you through the birth? Remember that the hospital midwife or nursing staff may be busy elsewhere from time to time, and that with a normal labour the doctor often arrives only in time to deliver the baby. Such a coach could be a childbirth educator, some of whom now specialise in birth counselling.

## PAIN RELIEF

Labour can be painful. You should have some knowledge of the various forms of pain relief available in childbirth, so that you can make an informed decision if a particular option is offered or needed. The main features of each are outlined below. You should discuss their pros and cons with your doctor well before the event.

### Psychoprophylaxis

This system, 'prepared childbirth', which is the basis of the antenatal classes at many hospitals, combines education, relaxation and exercise. You are taught about the processes of pregnancy and birth, to help eliminate your instinctive fears, and this knowledge is supplemented with specific breathing and muscular exercises for use at the different stages of labour. Psychoprophylaxis encourages the participation of a partner, and does not frown upon the use of other forms of pain relief.

# Tranquillisers

Tranquillisers such as diazepam (probably best known in the form of Valium) may be given in early labour. They have a calming effect and can help to counteract any urge to vomit; they may affect the baby by, for example, inhibiting the sucking reflex.

# Gas

This is a mix of nitrous oxide and oxygen, which you inhale through a mask. The gas is odourless and tasteless, has a mild effect (although it can make you feel fuzzy if you inhale too much), and is considered safe for both mother and baby. The procedure and timing will be explained to you at antenatal classes and by the midwife attending your birth: if you plan to use gas, practise applying the mask before the contractions become too strong. Its main disadvantage is that it is attached to the bedside and thus you can't walk around.

# Pethidine

Usually administered by injection, pethidine is a narcotic rather than a painkiller but is the most common means of pain relief in labour. It is usually administered after labour is well established, as it may inhibit contractions, but is generally not given too close to the stage when you need to be alert and able to push. The relief it provides varies greatly between women: it can take the edge off the pain, but its main benefit is that it allows you to relax or rest between contractions and thus conserve your energy for the birth itself. Pethidine can cause light-headedness and nausea in the mother. It may also cause drowsiness or respiratory depression in the baby, or interfere with her sucking reflex.

## Epidural anaesthetic

This is injected around the spinal cord, at about hip level, and numbs the body from the waist down. Relief lasts for several hours and can be extended with top-ups through a fine plastic tube. An epidural can make childbirth almost painless, although some women have experienced only patchy numbness. Its disadvantages are that it anchors you to the bed and is commonly accompanied by an intravenous drip.

## Nerve stimulation

Some hospitals now provide this option, which involves the use of a small gadget about the size of a beeper. It works on the premise that the small electrical waves it produces, and which you control, stimulate a barrier in the nervous system and block the sensation of pain being transmitted to the brain.

## Other options

There are various alternative methods of pain relief which you may wish to investigate. Self-hypnosis may help you to relax and distance yourself from the pain; it needs the right mental set, however, and lots of practice. Acupuncture and homoeopathy also offer possibilities. Ask your doctor for advice and contacts.

# BREAST OR BOTTLE?

Another decision facing you is how to feed your baby when she arrives. If you're unsure, discuss the facts and the arguments for and against with your doctor. You should also ask other mothers for their opinions, and – last but by no means least – discuss it with your partner, as his support will be indispensable. Today there is much pressure on mothers to breastfeed: if you opt for the bottle, or are unable to breastfeed, rest assured that your baby is just as likely to survive and thrive. Some of the pros and cons of both methods are outlined below.

## Breastfeeding

Breastfeeding is undoubtedly the best thing you can do for your baby and has many bonuses for you, the mother, too. The most common arguments in support of breastfeeding are that:

- breast milk is free, always available, always clean, and always at the perfect temperature
- breast milk contains antibodies that help protect your baby against infection
- breast milk is easy to digest, and less likely to cause diarrhoea or constipation
- unless you are expressing milk for storage, there is no need to sterilise bottles and teats
- breastfed babies are less likely to become overweight
- it allows mother and baby to share a special closeness
- it releases the hormone oxytocin, which helps the uterus to shrink more quickly.

Some of the arguments against breastfeeding are that:

■ your lifestyle and freedom are restricted, particularly during the first few months when your baby may require up to 12 feeds in 24 hours if you're feeding on demand

■ it's one aspect of parenting that you can't delegate to your partner

■ substances you eat, drink or smoke pass through the milk to the baby and you may have to adjust your intake accordingly

■ your wardrobe will be limited to easy-to-open tops as long as you breastfeed

■ you can't see how much milk your baby is getting

■ your milk supply may be affected by tiredness or stress.

Among the arguments for bottle-feeding are that:

■ other people can feed your baby

■ you can see exactly how much milk your baby is getting

■ you can wear what you like.

The arguments against bottle-feeding are that:

■ the milk formula and feeding equipment have to be bought

■ the bottles and teats have to be sterilised and the formula made up every day

■ outings require special containers to keep unused bottles cold and then warm them up

■ it takes time to warm a bottle, which is a particular chore in the dead of night

■ certain formulas may not suit your baby.

## CIRCUMCISION

Circumcision is the surgical removal of the foreskin of the penis. Some cultures practise circumcision as a religious ritual and it was adopted as routine practice, on hygienic grounds, in many western societies until quite recently. Today it is generally held that there are no valid medical reasons for circumcision, and the number of such operations has decreased to about 30 per cent (from a figure of about 70 per cent in the early 1980s). If undertaken, circumcision is performed under local or general anaesthetic, now more commonly at the age of about one year rather than in the early neonatal period. If you want your child to be circumcised, talk to your doctor: be prepared to be counselled against the operation.

## THE NAME GAME

Choosing a name for your baby can be great fun. The exercise of finding names that are acceptable to you and your partner (let alone to family and friends) can require lengthy debate and research, however, so it's best to start thinking as early as possible.

If you're short of ideas, there are quite a few books devoted to the subject, giving lists of names and their meanings. You could also check the birth notices of local papers to see which names are currently popular. Do consider any choices from all angles: names which are fashionable today may look very outdated in a few years time, and an exotic or unusual name may make your child the butt of jokes once she reaches school age. Also remember that Australians have a tendency to abbreviate names, so consider all the possible shortened versions.

# 4 ALL THE TRAPPINGS

~~~~~~~~~~~~~~~~~~~~~~~~~~~~

Some women start acquiring baby clothes and nursery equipment as soon as they know they're pregnant. Others leave it as late as possible, sometimes for superstitious reasons and sometimes simply because it's impossible to imagine what they'll really need (let alone the correct shapes or sizes).

The items listed below are those you will need in the first months after the baby is born (for maternity clothes, see chapter 2). Your experience as a mother (as remote as this may seem to you now) and new contacts you'll inevitably make once you become a parent will help shape your ideas and your later purchases, but some guidelines are included in case you like to plan or buy ahead.

Whether you're buying furniture, appliances or toys, check the label for a sticker from the Standards Association of Australia.

## Borrow or buy?

If you bought a comprehensive range of the baby goods available, you would need to add at least an extra room to the house. The solution? Borrow as many items as you can, particularly nursery furniture, as there are many items which have short-term use only and you'll be left with ever-increasing storage problems. Even if it's your first baby and you feel you'd like fresh new clothes, do consider accepting cast-offs: babies grow at a remarkable rate in the early months, so 'secondhand' items from this period have often had little use.

Also remember that you'll undoubtedly have at least a few friends and relatives eager to give you something for the baby. Booties and cardigans are particular favourites, so you could go light on these. From people you know well, particularly the grandparents-to-be, commission something specific from your list. There will still be plenty left for you to buy.

When you're buying, do watch for end-of-season sales. If this is likely to be the first of a number of pregnancies, buy the best quality goods you can afford because they will last longer. On the other hand, buy basics such as nappies, nighties, singlets and bibs from discount or chain stores. When furnishing the nursery, consider buying second-hand.

## FOR THE BABY

There are a number of basics that you should organise or buy in advance, as you'll need them from the time you go into hospital. Anyway, you'll find you won't get much done in the first few weeks after the baby is born.

### Basic checklist

Baby clothes for the first year are sized 000 (smallest), 00 and 0; some brands indicate weight and height as well, which is a help. Don't buy too many 000-sized items, as they are likely to be outgrown within weeks.

It is usually recommended that you wash new nappies and clothes before use, so that they are softer on the baby's skin. Where possible, choose those that are made of natural fibres (which are cooler in summer and warmer in winter), and are machine-washable, colour-fast, non-flammable, and easily fastened.

You will need the following:

- **4 or 5 singlets**. Cotton is usually sufficient as the baby is wrapped up snugly for the first few weeks, and size 00 is usually the safest unless you know your baby is likely to be particularly small or big.

- **5 or 6 nighties**. These tend to be worn day and night for the first few weeks, and are the most convenient clothing for quick nappy changes. Look for simple fastenings such as studs.

- **3 or 4 bunny rugs** (cotton or wool wraps). These are used to swaddle the baby in the first few weeks and can later be used as throw-overs for the pram, bassinet or stroller. Get a couple of different weights; avoid fancy fringes (that will tickle) and loose weaves (that little hands can push through).

- **36 cloth nappies** and 6 safety pins, if this is what you're planning to use (see below). Towelling nappies are more absorbent than cotton/flannel, but more difficult to fold to newborn size; prewashing may help. If you've opted for disposables, get in a good supply now (you'll need up to 70

a week in the first few months). Buy in bulk at supermarkets or discount stores, or try to find a wholesaler.
■ **4 or 5 pairs of pilchers** (pant-shaped nappy covers), if you're using cloth nappies. Those with velcro fasteners are easiest to adjust for size, and are more quickly fastened than those with studs.

## Optional extras
■ **2 or 3 jumpsuits**, with or without feet. These are useful for daywear after the first few weeks.
■ **jumpers or cardigans**. These are not essential, particularly in the early months when the baby is most commonly swaddled. If you want them, opt for natural fibres and easy fastenings.
■ **socks and booties**. These tend to be more trouble than they're worth. Socks are preferable, as they pull on easily but are hard to kick off; booties can look cute but tend to be flung off and can be a chore to tie on to kicking little feet.
■ **bonnets**. These are not really needed, although you will need a floppy hat to protect your baby's head in summer.

## WHICH SORT OF NAPPY?

Nappies will come to play a central role in your life – the hard facts are that you will change literally thousands of nappies in the next two or so years.

You can choose from several types of nappy, and your

choice will depend largely on your financial circumstances and the strength of your environmental conscience. The options are cloth nappies which you launder yourself, cloth nappies supplied and laundered by a nappy-wash service, or disposable nappies; many parents find that some combination of these is the best solution. If you can afford it (or can persuade a friend or relative to supply it as a present), do consider a nappy-wash service in the early months at least; there are many more rewarding ways that you can spend your time. The main pros and cons of each system are outlined below.

Cloth nappies:
- are reuseable (three dozen should last through two to three babies)
- are made of cotton (a natural fibre); *but*
- need to be soaked, rinsed and washed, a process which uses water and energy – both yours and the manufactured kind
- require folding (which can become boring on a daily basis) and pins (which tend to get lost and can inflict painful pricks).

Disposable nappies:
- are very convenient, as they're preshaped and thus don't require folding
- help prevent leaks, because they have a plastic outer layer; *but*
- are a continuing expenditure
- add to yours (and society's) waste problem

■ are usually bleached with chemicals, which can leach on to the baby's skin
■ tend to cause more nappy rash in babies than is the case with cloth nappies.

Nappy-wash services:
■ provide a regular supply of clean cloth nappies, and a bin to store the used ones in
■ spare you even rinsing soiled nappies.

Do your sums and weigh up the cost of each option, as only you know what value you put on your own time. Even if you decide on cloth nappies, it is worth keeping a supply of disposables to use on outings.

## FOR THE CAR

Today you are legally required to have an approved restraint for your baby in the car. The Safe'n Sound car 'capsule', while cumbersome, is the best in terms of safety, economy and space. Most restraints are costly, but they can be hired from many local councils: this is a sensible option, as they are only required for about six months. If you decide to hire one, reserve it as early as possible as there are often long waiting lists. A capsule comes with a bolt to anchor it into your car, so check whether you have the required hole (compulsory in recent car models), which is usually on the ledge behind the back seat.

Removable blinds for the car windows are a useful extra, as they help give the baby protection from the sun.

## FOR THE NURSERY

### Basic checklist
You will need the following:
- **a bassinet or basket**. You will use this for the first three or four months (or even longer, depending on its size). Plastic-covered, woven cane is preferable, as it allows air circulation and is easily cleaned.
- **bedding**. You'll need a well-fitting mattress (preferably new), a waterproof mattress cover, 3 or 4 bottom sheets (preferably fitted), 3 or 4 top sheets plus two blankets, or a duvet. As the bassinet is used for a relatively short time only, consider saving money by using cot-sized sheets and blankets folded in half. Alternatively, sheets and even blankets could be sewn quite easily, using new fabrics or unwanted larger bedlinen.
- **a mosquito net**. This is advisable in summer in most areas.
- **1 or 2 bathtowels**. These should be soft, but not necessarily baby-sized.
- **2 or more face washers**.
- **a nappy-changing table**. There is a bewildering variety available in the shops; alternatively, you could adapt an existing table or surface. You'll spend a lot of time at this table in the next couple of years, so whatever you use make

sure that it's at a comfortable height for you and your partner.

- **a chest of drawers**. This should be capable of taking all the baby's clothes and possibly her nappies. You might also consider a nappy hanger to save drawer space.

- **a pram or pram-stroller**. This is an expensive item and you should shop and ask around before making a decision. Are the handles the right height for you? Does it collapse quickly and easily for stowing in the car? Is it easy to push and steer? Is it well sprung? Does it have somewhere to stow your shopping? Does it have good brakes? Does it offer weather protection? A stroller with a lay-back seat is a good idea, as you can use it virtually from birth.

- **1 or 2 large nappy buckets**, with lids. Even if you intend to use disposable nappies, a nappy bucket is useful for soaking soiled clothes. A good supply of strong washing powder or nappy detergent is also invaluable.

- **toiletries**. Have on hand methylated spirits, a mild soap or bath solution, and baby shampoo. Also stock cotton balls or cotton wool, cotton buds, and plenty of tissues; pre-moistened wipes are also useful. Don't rush to buy appealing baby cosmetics as they will undoubtedly be accumulated along the way, with the first outbreak of nappy rash, cradle cap, eczema or dry skin. For summer babies, a total sunblock (factor 15+) is essential.

- **a baby bath**. You can choose from a portable plastic bath with or without a stand, or an inflatable bath. Alternatively, use the family bath or the laundry sink. Consider the baby's safety and your own comfort when choosing: avoid one which makes you bend uncomfortably, or is at a height or angle which gives you no control over the baby. Also remember that the bath has to be filled; one containing only a few centimetres of water is very heavy to carry. Various frames are available for supporting the baby in the bath, which can be very useful for unconfident parents as wet babies are disconcertingly slippery.

■ **a carry bag**. This should be big enough to hold all the items necessary for outings with the baby (nappies, spare clothes, tissues, bottle or cup). One which has pockets and sections is best from an organisational point of view; some also offer thermal containers for bottles. Unfortunately most are patterned for the baby's rather than the mother's enjoyment, so you may prefer to use a simple tote bag.

■ **a first-aid kit**. You should have a basic kit containing a thermometer, antiseptic, analgesic syrup or drops, blunt-ended scissors, tweezers and bandages.

■ **bottles, teats and formula**. One or two bottles are useful even if you're breastfeeding, as you may want to give your baby boiled water or an occasional bottle of formula. Ask your pharmacist or infant-welfare sister for advice when buying, although you may find your baby prefers one type of teat over another. You may also need to experiment with formulas, as some babies are allergic to certain mixtures.

■ **sterilising equipment**. Again, a basic kit is useful even if you're breastfeeding. There are many kinds available, probably the simplest of which is tablets which dissolve in water. All you then need is a roomy container (such as plastic cake bin) with a lid.

## Optional extras

- **nappy-change lotion**. This is pleasant to use but relatively costly on a regular basis. Plain water is the best alternative.
- **1 or 2 natural lambskins**. These will give you great service for years – in the pram or stroller, in the bassinet and cot, and on the floor.
- **a baby sling**. These enable you to keep your baby comfortable, warm and close, but leave your hands free. They can be a great way to get an unsettled baby to sleep.There are a number of different types available, from luxurious padded (but costly) versions to simple cloth affairs.
- **a nursery monitor**. This is an intercom with a portable receiver, which gives you freedom to move about the house or garden while your baby is asleep, in the confidence that you'll hear any squeaks or cries.
- **a baby bouncer** ('bouncinette'). This simple rocker with a harness is useful for rocking the baby gently while allowing her to look around. It can also double as a first high chair.
- **a night light or dimmer switch** in the nursery. This is very useful for night feeds or visits. It's also worth leaving a comfortable chair in the nursery for the same purpose.
- **nappy liners** (either disposable or reusable). These are simply cloth or plastic triangles which are used to catch, and thus easily remove, bowel products.

## Toys

Irresistible as they may be, a baby really needs very few toys in the early months. If you can't resist the temptation, remember that most objects tend to be explored by mouth during the first year, so consider sturdy items and non-toxic finishes.

The most useful and long-lived buys at this stage are mobiles, which can be suspended above the bassinet (later moving to the cot) and change table. Also worth considering is an inexpensive string-pull music box, which is a useful soother and can from the earliest days become part of the sleeptime ritual.

Babies don't respond much to soft toys during the first year; after about three or four months, however, provide small colourful objects to hold, bang and shake. You'll find a wealth of these in your kitchen cupboards, so don't buy too many as they tend to have a relatively short life.

## Planning ahead

If you have the time or the inclination, it is worth thinking a bit ahead about the things you'll need later in the first year. Buying in advance, particularly at sales, can save you quite a lot of money.

In the longer term you'll need the following:

■ **a cot** (any time from about four months). When buying a cot, considering safety first, then comfort. Like prams, cots can be costly but it's worth buying well because it will be used for two to three years. Check the distance between the slats, (make sure a baby's head can't fit through), the position of the hinges (placed just where little fingers could undo them?), its sturdiness (even a year-old baby can rattle the bars with surprising force), and the quality of the mattress. A cot bumper (a padded strip which lines the bars) will help protect the baby's head as she becomes more active.

■ **a portable cot**. This will be useful if you plan to spend much time away from home with the baby. It should be light, have the same safety characteristics as a proper cot, and be easily folded and stored. A jointed 'fence' is now available, which can be folded to form either a playpen or cot and thus makes a useful dual-purpose alternative.

■ **a high chair**. This will be needed from about five to six months. You can choose from the traditional freestanding types or one of the collapsible models that are attached to the table. Consider safety aspects such as safety belts, movable bits that might crunch fingers, stability, and ease of cleaning.

■ **a playpen**. Depending on the layout of your house, you may want to be able to enclose your baby while you're busy elsewhere. There are many types available: again consider sturdiness, and safety factors such as wood splinters, paint surface, and so on.

■ **a car seat**. You'll need this from about four to six months. As with baby capsules there are basic safety requirements, so get an approved model.

## OTHER THINGS TO THINK ABOUT

Buying clothes and furniture is just one part of preparing your house for the arrival of a baby. Other matters worth considering ahead are outlined below.

## Saving labour

If you don't have them already, there are a few labour-saving devices which you should consider if you can afford them. First on the list is undoubtedly an automatic washing machine: even if you aren't washing nappies, it is remarkable how much washing is generated by one small baby several times a week. A tumble dryer is also a boon, particularly in winter.

A microwave oven will probably also look like less of a luxury once you're at home with your baby, as it dramatically reduces the amount of time you devote to both cooking and reheating food. It is not advisable to use a microwave for warming bottles, however, as the contents can quickly beome overhot although the bottle itself remains cool to the touch.

## Safety

Babies don't move around much at all in the first few months. Right from the beginning, however, there are a number of precautions you'll need to take. Once your baby is on the move (crawling starts any time from about eight months), little in your home can be considered safe. It is sensible to consider taking a brief course in first aid, or at least to learn techniques such as artificial respiration and how to cope with bleeding, choking, burns and electric shocks.

- **Heating**. Babies need to be kept fairly warm and at as even a temperature as possible. Any heating appliance used in the nursery should be out of the baby's reach; avoid oil or kerosene heaters, which emit quite powerful fumes. Electric blankets should not be used for a baby or small child.

- **Ventilation**. The baby's room should be well ventilated, but avoid direct draughts near the bassinet or cot. Fans, like heaters, should have a childproof grille or be kept out of reach.
- **Doors and windows**. If you like leaving windows and doors open for fresh air, insect screens are advisable. Late in the first year you may need to consider chocks or guards to prevent doors slamming on little fingers, adjustable barriers for doorways and stairs, and childproof locks on doors and windows.
- **Furniture**. Check all your furniture for sharp edges, finishes that may be dangerous if chewed, wood splinters, and so on. Once your baby is crawling, put any unstable items (or dangerous objects on low surfaces) out of reach.
- **Cupboards and drawers**. These are a treasure trove for inquisitive babies. Once your baby is crawling, cupboard doors and drawers may need to be made childproof; any dangerous objects (glassware, knives, forks, scissors) and substances (medications, cleaning agents) should be kept out of reach.
- **Floors**. Any carpet in the nursery should be easy to clean. Have a minumum of slippery surfaces, for both yours and the baby's sake.

## Convenience

While it's fun to make the nursery comfortable and attractive, don't clutter it up too much in the early days as you'll find that you accumulate many new 'essentials' in the first months.

There are a number of ways in which you can make your life easier.

■ **Storage**. You will need a surprising amount of storage space in the nursery: for clothes, nappies, bedding, rugs and shawls, toiletries, and possibly even the pram-stroller attachments. Drawers are more useful than hanging space in the first year; you'll also need somewhere to store the outgrown clothes of the first few months, which accumulate at quite a rate.

■ **Nappy-changing needs**. It's vital to have nappies, tissues and lotions close to the change table, as some active babies make it dangerous for you to turn your back even for ten seconds. Open shelves or a stack of three to four wire baskets are preferable, as you can see and reach everything easily.

# 5 THE TIME IS NEARING

At about 30 weeks your delivery date still seems a long way away. In the last month or two, especially if you're feeling uncomfortable and are able to do less than usual, you may well feel bored and restless. Don't get too impatient, however. If you're well and the baby is well, be prepared to wait until nature takes its course.

## MAKING GOOD USE OF THE LAST WEEKS

Use the last weeks to ensure that you and your house are fully prepared (see chapter 4), to get some extra rest if possible, and even to pamper yourself a bit. Difficult as it may be for first-time mothers to imagine, there won't be much spare time to get things done in the first weeks after the baby is born.

### Stock up ahead

Depending on the cooking abilities of your partner, it may be wise to prepare some meals to tide the household over during and after your stay in hospital. An easy way to do this is to double the quantities for two or three meals a week, and freeze the surplus.

If finances permit, stock up at the supermarket on non-perishables, particularly bulky items such as soap powder, tissues, toilet paper, pet food, and so on. Check whether your regular supermarket makes home deliveries, which will be particularly useful once you've a baby to carry as well. They may even accept phone orders.

Buy in advance any birthday or Christmas presents, if you're due at these times. Consider buying a small gift for your partner, as you and the baby are likely to be showered with gifts and attention and he may feel left out.

## Do some spring-cleaning

An urge to 'nest-build' often comes over many women in late pregnancy. If you have the time, and your condition permits, this may well be a good time to tackle some of those once-a-decade jobs such as cleaning the windows, mending and sorting clothes, washing curtains and covers, and getting rid of excess dust and cobwebs. Don't overdo it, however, and avoid precarious places such as ladders.

Prepare the baby's room or sleeping area. Make up the cot or bassinet, hang a mobile, and add a frieze or other inexpensive splash of colour to the walls. Wash the baby's clothes and organise the nappy-change area.

## Other practical things to do

If you're handy about the house, consider fitting the baby capsule into the car. (It is most important to follow the manufacturer's directions exactly.) If you have any doubts, check with more experienced parents or with your local council if the capsule has been hired.

Put a waterproof sheet over your mattress, in case your waters break while you're in bed.

Read as much as possible about new babies and, if relevant, about breastfeeding. Contact the Nursing Mothers' Association to find out about the many services they offer, and consider introducing yourself to your local infant-welfare sister.

If you have some spare time, consider doing a short course in sewing or first aid.

Sort out your financial situation and make sure that all outstanding bills are paid.

Ask about the neighbourhood for any experienced baby-sitters. It's never too early to find a reliable, likeable and not-too expensive one.

If you haven't done so already, find out about any home-help provided by your local council, or organise a house-cleaner for a few hours each week.

If your hospital offers no domiciliary care, ask your doctor or midwife about any organisations in your area that might provide this (generally inexpensive) service. For the first few weeks, you may find it more convenient to have a midwife call on you than to go to the infant-welfare centre.

## SPEND SOME TIME ON YOURSELF

You will find you have little or no leisure time in the first weeks at home. There are quite a few things worth doing now:

- have a haircut
- have a legwax or facial
- visit your dentist
- see a film
- have a relaxed coffee, lunch or drink with a friend.

This is also a good time to investigate your wardrobe. Resurrect some pre-pregnancy outfits, but don't expect to be able to wear close-fitting clothes straight after the birth as your body may take several months to regain its old shape. Buy a new item of clothing, if you can afford it .

## WHAT TO PACK FOR HOSPITAL

You should pack your hospital bag well ahead of your due date, in case your baby is early. In the last few weeks, if you're travelling far by car, take the bag with you just in case.

Your hospital will probably give you a list of things you should take for you and the baby. Some tend to overestimate what's required: if your partner is likely to visit daily, don't forget that he can do some clothes washing for you and bring anything you've forgotten.

The checklist below includes the basics for you and the baby, as well as some suggestions for extras that may be useful.

### For you
- **nighties or pyjamas**. Take 2 or 3, remembering to have a comfortable outfit for the birth itself and save your best one

for afterwards. If you're planning to breastfeed, choose nighties or tops that open to the waist. Hospitals are air-conditioned, so a light fabric such as cotton will probably do. Beware of synthetic fabrics that store static electricity, as they will cling to every not-so-slinky curve.

■ **a dressing-gown and slippers**. You will probably spend quite a bit of time out of your room – visiting the nursery, attending postnatal exercise classes or strolling to the hospital shop – and many hospitals require these for modesty's sake.

■ **underpants**. Take several pairs, as you may need more than one change a day because of postnatal bleeding. Disposable pants are worth considering.

■ **2 or 3 nursing bras**, if you plan to breastfeed. Also include a box of nursing pads to absorb any leaks.

■ **sanitary pads**, for postnatal bleeding. These may be supplied by the hospital for the first few days, but after that it's usually your responsibility. Buy the 'super' size, and also consider the adhesive kind as they are probably the most convenient.

■ **toiletries and cosmetics**. The basics are toothbrush, hair-brush, deodorant and make-up. Also take a moisturiser, as the air-conditioned hospital environment can be very drying and your lips may be sore after the exertions of labour. Other useful items are perfumed wipes or a bottle of cologne, which are good refreshers.

■ **clothes**. Some hospitals encourage you to get dressed during the day, and you'll need an outfit to wear home.

Some also encourage you and your partner to have an evening out during your stay.

- **money**. You may need some small change to use the public telephone, buy a newspaper or magazine, raid the hospital shop, and buy something for the nurses on your floor.

- **writing material and address book**. You may want to let distant family and friends know about the arrival, and may also find time to write some thank-you letters. It's worth considering starting a diary, as you will find that you forget many details of the early days and it can give you much pleasure and amusement in years to come.

- **reading matter**. If you opt for a book it should be something light, as hospitals and babies are notorious for noise, interruptions and distractions.

- **a radio or cassette-player**. Music can provide useful distraction during labour, as well as afterwards. Take headphones if you've got them, and don't forget a favourite tape or two.

- **a camera and/or video**. Although your baby won't be doing very much in the first days, you'll treasure your first family snaps.

- **champagne**, for that first celebration after the birth.

## For the baby
The amount you require for your baby varies between hospitals. You will generally need the following:
- **several cotton singlets** (size 00 is safest)
- **several nighties**

- **several bunny rugs**
- **nappies** (plus safety pins for cloth nappies)
- **a going-home outfit**, if you want something special.

See chapter 4 for more details and guidelines.

## THE BIRTH-DAY BLUEPRINT

It's a good idea to clarify in your mind (and even write down) a birth-day strategy – your plans for labour and the birth (preferred delivery position, pain relief and so on) assuming that everything progresses normally. You should also establish your preferences in the event of a caesarean birth being required. Do you, for example, want your partner present? Do you want an epidural (which allows you to be awake throughout) rather than a general anaesthetic, if it's not an emergency?

At the same time, be prepared to be flexible and to be guided by the advice of the nursing staff and your doctor. After all, that's why they're there.

### List of contacts

Keep a note, on your fridge or near the phone, of such details as the following:

- name, address (including Melways reference) and phone number of the hospital, birthing centre, or other proposed venue for the birth
- name and phone number of your doctor

■ a contact number for your partner and for anyone else who is attending the birth.

## Transport to the hospital

Work out the quickest route to the hospital or birthing centre, and how long it takes (in both peak and offpeak traffic).

If your partner is unable to drive you, consider how you will get there. Caution suggests you would be unwise to drive yourself: those mild contractions are sure to have more bite once you're behind the wheel and could take the edge off your driving skills. Consider a friend or a taxi instead.

## HOSPITAL PROCEDURES TO THINK ABOUT

In addition to preparing for the birth itself, find out about your hospital's procedures and practices, as you may wish to discuss these in advance.

## Pre-birth shaving and enema

It was once routine practice to shave the mother's pubic area and give her an enema before the birth, but many hospitals now give you a choice in the matter. Shaving is generally considered to be an unnecessary indignity, unless there is excessive hair around the perineum. An enema to clear out your bowels is well worth considering, however, as it helps to make room in the pelvis and can prevent the embarrassment of opening your bowels when you are pushing to deliver the baby.

## Disposal of the placenta

Some couples now opt to perform a ritual disposal of the placenta that has nourished their baby for so long. If this is your choice, you should discuss the matter with the hospital in advance.

## Rooming in

Assuming you and your baby are well after the birth, you can opt to have her in your room 24 hours a day while you're in hospital. Many hospitals encourage mothers to do this, as it makes demand feeding easier and helps the mother to get to know and to practise caring for her baby from the start. Particularly if the birth is tiring, however, you may wish to consider leaving your baby in the nursery for some or all of the night, so that you can get some rest.

## Dummies (or 'pacifiers')

Some hospitals routinely use dummies to soothe unsettled babies, so you should make your preferences clear in this matter beforehand. Dummies tend to go in and out of fashion, and like thumb-sucking have generated quite heated debate over the years. Those in favour of dummies argue that sucking is a natural infant reflex and that many babies need extra sucking; a dummy can provide an important source of comfort and security for grizzling or unhappy babies until they 'find their thumbs'. Those opposed to the use of dummies argue that they are unhygienic if not kept clean, tend to drop out periodically and thus require parental vigilance, and can establish 'bad habits' of dependency.

# 6 LABOUR AND THE BIRTH

~~~~~~~~~~~~~~~~

There are various signs which may indicate that labour is not too far away. Two of the most common are mild diarrhoea and a sudden burst of enthusiasm for nest-building – vacuuming, decorating, or watering the garden.

However much you've read about or discussed childbirth, the first signs of true labour tend to be regarded with doubt or disbelief. Most women are anxious not to make fools of themselves by raising a false alarm – was that really a contraction, or was it just wind? Don't hesitate to contact your hospital or midwife at any time, if only to give yourself peace of mind.

## LABOUR: TRUE OR FALSE?

Every mother is likely to have a slightly different story about how her labour started and progressed. As you will have learnt in your antenatal classes, there are several important signs to look for and it is most likely that one of the three following things will happen.

### A discharge (or 'show') of mucus from the vagina
This means that the plug blocking the cervical canal since the beginning of your pregnancy has been dislodged, which is

usually caused by contractions dilating the cervix. The discharge is usually jelly-like, and often tinged with traces of blood. Unless it is accompanied by other signs of labour, there is no need for any action as labour may still be days away.

## Your 'waters' may break

This means that the amniotic sac in which the baby is floating has ruptured. The resulting fluid is clear or slightly blood-flecked; it may appear in a gush, or there may be just a trickle. Whatever the case you will have no control over the leak, no matter how hard you squeeze your pelvic muscles.

When your waters break, even if there are no further signs of labour, you should contact your hospital or midwife as the baby's protective envelope has gone and there is some risk of infection. It is not uncommon, however, for women to lose their waters without noticing it or for the waters not to break until towards the end of the first stage of labour.

## Contractions may start

A contraction has many guises. It may feel like a stomach cramp or period pain, or be associated more with backache. The pang may not even raise an eyebrow, or it may be forceful enough to rouse you from a deep sleep. For such a pain to be a true contraction, however, it must be repeated (whether in 20 minutes or 100 minutes) and gradually gain in intensity and recur more frequently. Although most women find that contractions eventually follow a reasonably regular pattern, some find them totally without order – one contraction may follow hard on the heels of another and then all may be quiet for 20 minutes.

## Time to go?

If any of these signs appear, contact your hospital or midwife. They will most likely recommend that you stay at home for the moment, unless the contractions are regular (about every eight minutes) or are becoming quite uncomfortable, or something unusual, such as bleeding, occurs.

Once labour is diagnosed, make sure that your hospital bag is ready and alert your partner. Try to stay relaxed, but keep busy until the action heats up: go for a walk, visit a friend, or invite a friend over if you are by yourself. Run your mind over the birth blueprint, and proceed with any arrangements for transport to the hospital. While you still have time, consider a shower in the comfort of your own bathroom.

## INDUCED BIRTHS: WHAT HAPPENS?

Your doctor may decide to start labour artificially to protect you or your baby. The most common reasons for induction are medical disorders such as diabetes or high blood pressure, the baby being very overdue, or evidence that the placenta is no longer providing adequate nourishment. Induction should not be performed routinely just because the baby is late, however, or for the convenience of you or your doctor. If induction is advised in your case, make sure that there are good medical grounds.

If your baby is to be induced, you will probably be admitted to hospital the night before. Even if you have booked a private room you may spend this night in a preparatory ward, so take some good music or reading matter to take your mind off both the wait ahead and the goings-on around you. In the morning your doctor will make a vaginal examination to determine how far your cervix has softened ('ripened') in preparation for the birth.

The most common induction techniques are rupturing the amniotic sac artificially or administering the hormone oxytocin (which stimulates contractions) by means of an intravenous drip. Ask for the drip to be mounted on a portable stand, so that you have some freedom to move around in the early stages of labour. Contractions usually begin quite quickly, but tend to be more intense; induction does increase the likelihood of intra-uterine foetal monitoring, a forceps delivery and an episiotomy.

## ARRIVING AT THE HOSPITAL

As soon as you've rung the hospital to let them know that labour has started, the reception staff will be expecting you. Once you have given your name at the desk there is usually some paperwork to be done, with admission forms to fill in giving details such as your medical history, next-of-kin and so on. If you're married but are commonly known by your maiden name, give the reception desk both surnames so as to avoid confusion when friends telephone or visit.

You will then be taken or directed to the maternity section. The admitting sister will assess the progress of labour by asking relevant questions, taking your pulse, temperature and blood pressure, and timing contractions and checking their intensity. A brief pelvic examination may follow to ascertain how far your cervix has dilated; the baby's heartbeat may also be checked. If everything is in order, your doctor will probably be notified about your admission.

You will now be asked for your baby's clothes (unless they are supplied by the hospital), given a shave or enema if desired, offered a shower, and given the chance to change into whatever you've chosen to wear for the birth. You may of course elect to wear nothing, although some hospitals may be disconcerted by this if you are likely to be roaming the corridors.

Throughout this period, partners are often neglected. Keep him close at hand, if that's what you both want. If you're feeling too apprehensive or uncomfortable to assert yourself, let him do the talking if he's aware of your wishes. Remain flexible, however, and be guided by the professional advice you receive. Don't be afraid to ask questions or to query any procedure that you don't understand.

## The labour ward

If you have toured a labour ward during your antenatal classes, you will be at least a little familiar with the layout and atmosphere. Compared to the informal atmosphere of a birthing centre, a labour ward is fairly clinical and impersonal, with lots of chrome appliances and few home comforts. There is usually a special delivery bed, which can be shortened, raised and lowered; nearby are arranged special lighting, a gas mask, a drip set up on a stand, a foetal heart monitor, trolleys containing bowls, basins and medical equipment, and a bassinet containing clothing for the baby. Don't be put off or intimidated by all this gadgetry, as not all of it is necessarily brought into play.

## BIRTH – A THREE-PART STORY

An average birth takes anywhere from five to 24 hours. There are two main stages involved, although birth is traditionally described as a three-part process which includes the delivery of the placenta after the baby is born.

### The first stage
During the first stage of labour, your contractions become stronger and more frequent as the cervix dilates and the baby is propelled down the birth canal. This stage lasts, on average, anywhere between four and 14 hours.

The progress of the contractions is measured in fingers or centimetres, by pelvic examinations; at 10 centimetres, the cervix is considered fully dilated. The process is not necessarily evenly timed: you may be in labour for six hours with seemingly little progress made, then the bulk of the dilating work may be done in an intense 30 minutes.

Towards the end of this stage, when the cervix is nearly open, is often described as the 'transition phase'. The contractions tend to be more painful, and you may feel the urge to push your baby out (rather like an uncontrollable need to open your bowels). It is important not to push until your doctor tells you to, because pushing before the cervix is fully dilated can bring the danger of tearing your perineum as well as applying excessive pressure on the baby. As you draw towards the end of the first stage of labour, you will be checked more regularly by the nursing staff.

## The second stage
This phase of labour, which begins once the cervix is fully open, produces the baby. It lasts anywhere between 45 minutes and three hours for first-time mothers and 15 to 45 minutes for the 'old hands'.

Once your cervix is fully dilated, the process of pushing out the baby begins. Your doctor will advise you when to push: during each effort, hold your breath briefly (and only briefly, or both you and the baby could be robbed off oxygen) and tense your body from the waist down. Once the head is delivered the hardest part is done, and the baby's shoulders and body are guided out with a minimum of effort on your part. If you're up to it, do try to watch the delivery, either directly or with the aid of a mirror– it really is worthwhile.

## The third stage
The final stage of the birth, in which the placenta is expelled, usually lasts little longer than 20 minutes.

An injection of synotocinon is often given routinely, to hasten the ejection of the placenta and so reduce blood loss.

Some experts now question the need for this artificial stimulus, however, so discuss the matter with your doctor or midwife. In the rare event that the placenta does not come away of its own accord, it must be removed manually.

## WHAT TO EXPECT AND WHAT TO DO

In the early stages of labour you may see a lot or only a little of the midwives on duty, depending on how many other mothers-to-be are in labour, how advanced your labour is, and how normal your condition. If you are largely being left to your own devices and your partner is not there yet, you may feel lonely. Check with the midwife and go for a walk around the corridors, look at the babies in the nursery, talk to some other mothers-in-waiting, watch some television, or telephone a friend. The walking and the diversion will benefit you.

You should also be prepared for changes of staff during your labour as shifts come and go, resulting in a temporary loss of continuity. Unless there are unforeseen complications, your doctor will probably not arrive until the first stage of labour is nearly over. Her arrival tends to be greeted with a good deal of relief as it is a signal that the end is in sight.

If possible, try to remain upright during the first stage of labour, as once you're lying down it can be hard to get up again. Stay relaxed and mobile if possible, so that gravity can play its part. Try not to fight the contractions, relax into them instead. If you're up to it, a warm shower or bath is soothing at this stage and will help your muscles go about their business more efficiently. Even the humble hot-water bottle can provide relief, especially if you're experiencing a lot of back pain.

Discuss pain relief as you go along. Some pain relief measures need to be synchronised with the various stages of labour, so make sure that staff know what you want.

Your partner should be both your ally and your advocate. He can be involved by massaging your back or perineum, by encouraging you to stay mobile, and by keeping you supplied with water if your mouth becomes dry. If you have decided on a squatting or kneeling position, he can help support you.

Some of the more common problems and procedures associated with labour and birth are outlined below.

## Panic

During the first stage of labour it is not unusual to feel panic. Talk about any such feelings with your partner or your doctor, and do some deep breathing to steady yourself. In extreme cases, tranquillisers may be used.

## Vomiting

Depending on the intensity of the pain, and when you last ate, you may vomit. There should enough warning for you to request a bowl.

## Fatigue

You may experience waves of great tiredness, if the first stage of labour is very long or if you are subject to periods of irregular but intense contractions that leave you little time to rest in between. If you feel yourself getting very tired, try to eat or drink something and take a shower or bath. If all else fails consider some pain relief, because it is important to save some energy to push out your baby.

## Slow or ineffective labour

If labour progresses very slowly, or if your contractions appear to be ineffectual, labour can be speeded up by an enema, by a shower, or by walking. Further measures include breaking your waters or administering the hormone oxytocin by intravenous drip. As synthetic oxytocin makes contractions more forceful it can shorten labour, but the pain is likely to be more intense.

## Foetal heart monitoring

If your baby is thought to be in distress, you may be linked up to a monitor which records the baby's heartbeat. The monitor will be passed into your vagina and attached to the baby's head, which means that you will be anchored to the bed.

## Baby positioned awkwardly

If the baby's head is facing your abdomen, rather than your side or back as is normally the case, you may feel a great deal of back pain. If your doctor ascertains that your baby is lying in a breech position (bottom rather than head down), it is sometimes possible to turn her. If not, a normal delivery may still be possible, although an episiotomy or even a caesarean may be necessary, especially for first-time mothers.  If the baby is lying across the uterus or shoulder-first, a caesarean birth is usually required.

## Opening your bowels

The effort of pushing to expel your baby can cause you to open your bowels involuntarily. Although embarrassing to anticipate, such an event is in fact scarely noticeable amid all the goings-on and the staff are well prepared to remove the products immediately.

## Feeling disheartened

If there are any problems or complications during labour, technology may be brought into play. Unexpectedly being attached to a drip or requiring pain relief can be disappointing if you were hoping for a natural birth. The best thing to do is to have a cry if you feel like it, but remember that childbirth is not a matter of success or failure – undoubtedly such procedures are in the best interests of you and your baby.

## Episiotomy

Episiotomy is a cut made in the area between the vagina and anus (called the perineum) to make delivery of the baby's head easier and avoid the skin tearing. This may be deemed necessary if the opening is too small, or if the baby needs to be manually rotated or removed with forceps. An episiotomy is painless, as a local anaesthetic is given and the region is already relatively numb through stretching.

## Forceps delivery

Forceps may be used to draw down the baby's head, if the baby is stuck in the birth canal, needs to be rotated, or is in distress.

A local anaesthetic and an episiotomy are usually required for such a delivery. Forceps may cause some bruising on the baby's head, but this will disappear within a few days.

## Caesarean birth

A caesarean 'section', in which the baby is removed from the womb via a cut made through the mother's abdomen, may be performed for a number of reasons. It may be planned during pregnancy if, for example, you have a medical disorder such as diabetes, heart disease or genital herpes, if the baby's head is too large for your pelvic opening, or if the baby is badly positioned and cannot be turned. During labour, an emergency caesarean may be deemed necessary if you or the baby are in distress, if labour is too prolonged, if an induction has failed to produce effective labour, or in the event of a crisis such as a prolapsed umbilical cord (where the cord drops down first and threatens to cut off the baby's circulation).

A caesarean involves a 10–12 centimetre cut made just below the bikini line. If it is an emergency operation, a general anaesthetic is given. If not, you may opt for an epidural anaesthetic so that you are awake for the delivery; your partner will also be allowed to remain at your side.

## AFTER THE BIRTH – THE FIRST MOMENTS

Unless there are complications, the baby is usually lifted on to your abdomen straight after the delivery and the umbilical cord is clamped and cut. Some experts now suggest that the cord-cutting be delayed until either the placenta separates or the cord stops pulsating, as this allows the baby to continue receiving maternal oxygen until its own breathing apparatus takes over.

Immediately after the birth, you will be given a quick clean-up. If you have had an episiotomy, it will be stitched while the area is still numb from the local anaesthetic. The baby's nose and mouth are usually suctioned to prevent any remaining fluid being inhaled, and then routine checks are made to ensure that everything is there, normal and working.

You and your partner will probably be invited to observe any tests made on the baby, which should be kept to a minimum at this stage. To confirm that your baby is adapting to life outside the womb, checks are made regularly in the first minutes after the birth: these assess the baby's heart rate, breathing, colour, and reflex responses. Don't be too anxious about the score – you'll know if there are any problems – but do ask if you're interested.

Routine checks will also be made on your blood pressure, pulse and temperature. Unless there have been any complications, all three of you will then probably be left alone to rest and to get to know each other. If you're planning to breastfeed, this is a good time to let your baby feed for a few minutes. This not only brings you a special feeling of intimacy, but also releases the pituitary hormone oxytocin which both stimulates milk production and helps the uterus to shrink.

In the event of complications, your baby may be removed to the special-care nursery soon after the birth. If this is the case, or if you are in pain, feeling exhausted, or fighting the after-effects of medication, don't worry if you don't cuddle or breast-feed your baby immediately. A few hours separation will have no devastating long-term effects on her, or on the 'bonding' process.

## What about you?

After some time alone with your baby, you and your partner may want to start making phone calls to family and friends, or you may just want to rest. Depending on your condition, you may be encouraged to shower and go to the toilet or you may be given a more thorough sponge-wash. Afterwards it's off to your room, or the staff depart if you're in a birthing centre. During this time your baby may be checked more thoroughly, possibly by a paediatrician, and washed and dressed for the first time. If you want to keep your baby with you, however, do say so – a wash can wait.

Depending on many factors – not least the rigours of the birth – you may experience a rush of love or a rush of relief when you first take your baby in your arms. You may feel elated, stunned, or simply worn out, and if your baby has been removed to the nursery you may also feel a great sense of anti-climax.

## YOUR BABY: EARLY IMPRESSIONS

At last your baby is a real, live parcel in your arms. Many first-time parents get something of a shock when they see their newborn, which invariably bears little resemblance to the plump, pink babies of advertising catalogues. There are a few characteristics common to most newborn babies, which – rest assured – are temporary defects only and will disappear within weeks. If your baby is alert and all the tests indicate everything is normal, there is nothing to worry about, but do check with staff if it makes you feel easier.

## Hair and eyes

Most newborn babies arrive with similar bluish-grey eyes, and well-formed nails on toes and fingers. They vary widely as to the amount and colour of hair, however, and this is no accurate guide to their future appearance.

## Umbilical stump

After the cord is cut and clamped. your baby will be left with a longish, often bloodied, stub with a peg-like clip on it. This will shrivel and fall off within a week or so. The area should be cleaned with methylated spirits at least twice a day until the area is quite clean and dry.

## Head shape

A newborn baby's head is very large in proportion to the rest of her body. It may be elongated, pointed or otherwise oddly shaped, because the skull bones remain soft to allow the head to be moulded for its movement down the narrow birth canal. Her head may also be bruised as the result of its squeezed journey out of the womb, and perhaps from the use of forceps.

You will also notice a soft spot – known as the fontanelle – at the top of the head, which will gradually disappear over the next few months as the bones draw together.

## Skin colour

Your baby may look quite dark, even bluish, immediately after the birth until oxygen is taken in. The skin may be covered with some blood, with a greasy protective substance known as vernix, and with fine white hairs ('lanugo') that will disappear in a month.

Your baby may also be a little yellow, which is a sign of jaundice (a build-up of bile in the blood). This usually disappears within a few days, but if not mild treatment (in the form of exposure to a bright blue light) may be given.

## Genitals and breasts

The genitals may look disproportionately large and may be swollen. In females, there may also be some vaginal discharge as the mother's hormones are gradually withdrawn. The breasts may also be swollen.

## Spots and rashes

There may be tiny white or yellowish spots under the skin, particularly around the bridge of the nose. These are called milia and are caused by the skin glands unplugging themselves. Red blotches, spots and rashes are also common, and usually disappear as quickly as they appeared.

## Birth marks

There are many different birth marks, some of which simply result from prominent blood vessels and fade within the first year or so.

# 7 HOSPITAL DAZE

## THE NEW YOU: OUCH!

The day after the birth, your baby is only 12 hours old but you feel as if you have aged many years. You look down at your abdomen and wonder about that mound of spongy flesh: could there be another baby still in there? You're bruised and possibly stitched into the bargain, and the mere thought of a trip to the loo brings tears to the eye. Hormones are running rampant, and your body and brain may be confused. Your main solace, apart from your baby, is the knowledge that the other women in your room or in adjoining rooms are shuffling to the same postnatal beat.

You'll undoubtedly find that the thought of walking is worse than the act. A shower will make you feel a lot better, and it may be the best place to try to urinate for the first time, especially if you've had stitches, as it will reduce the stinging. A clean body, clean hair and a clean outfit will make you feel at least like a newer person. Activity and walking, and pelvic floor exercises, will also help bruises and swelling to disappear more quickly.

## COMMON PROBLEMS

### Aches and pains
Depending on the ease or otherwise of the birth, you may have a sore chest and dry lips from the exertions of labour. If you have had a forceps delivery or episiotomy, your bottom may well be sore. You may be also feel 'afterpains' for days or even weeks, as your uterus shrinks back to its former size.

### Stitches
If you have had an episiotomy, ask about a salt bath if it hasn't already been suggested: the salt will help the stitches to dry more quickly, and a bath is relaxing. Try to take three a day. Ice packs may provide some relief, and a rubber ring (usually supplied by the hospital on request), can make sitting more comfortable.

If you've had a caesarean, your stitched abdomen may make it uncomfortable to move and to breastfeed. Pain-relief tablets may be required.

### Postnatal bleeding
As your uterus shrinks and crumbles, there will be a bloody discharge (known as lochia) from your vagina for several days. The discharge may continue for up to six weeks, fading to brownish after the first week and thereafter to a yellowish-white. A good supply of sanitary pads is your best defence, and tampons should not be used until your doctor advises otherwise.

# DAILY LIFE

Hospitals run to a schedule, and you and your baby will be fitted as neatly as possible into it. If you're well, you'll be asked to vacate your bed at about the same time each day so that it can be changed or remade, meals will be delivered at set times, and routine checks will be made on you morning and evening.

Usually there is a designated time set aside each day for bathing the baby, and a quiet time when visitors and telephone callers are discouraged. As hospital life can be hectic, with your baby to feed and care for as well as visitors pouring in and out, you will probably be grateful for some order being imposed.

## The nursing staff

The hospital staff is there to help and advise you, so do ask them about anything that concerns you. They will teach you basics such as how to change nappies, burp and bath your baby, and clean the umbilical stump. While you may be grateful for some help and advice, remember that this instruction is intended to provide guidelines only and you may find that you devise your own systems once you're back in your own home.

You may get conflicting advice and opinions from the nurses on different shifts, which can be confusing for inexperienced mothers. If this happens, you will have to abide by your instinctive feelings to some extent. If you have any serious worries or questions, make sure that you get adequate answers.

## Your doctor

If your delivery was normal, your doctor may pay you only fleeting visits. Capture her if you have any queries about the birth, your present condition or any other matter.

## Visitors

Visits from your partner and close family are allowed outside regular hours in most hospitals. Mothers and babies tend to attract a lot of visitors, to the extent that your room may resemble a party during visiting hours. This can be tiring, however, and in the early days many new mothers feel self-conscious about feeding or changing their baby in public. Do let the staff know if you don't feel like visitors, although it may be more tactful to ask friends and relatives to telephone before they plan to come.

## Classes

There are usually a number of classes on offer during your hospital stay, for postnatal exercises and bottle-feeding procedures. It's worthwhile attending the latter even if you are breastfeeding. Before you leave hospital, also ask to be shown how to express milk from your breasts, either by hand or using one of the special-purpose pumps that are available. This means that you can store your milk and have some time off while someone else feeds your baby.

## Rooming in

The presence of your baby well may help you to forget your own physical state. If, on the other hand, you've opted to have your baby with you all the time but find it difficult to sleep because of the squeaks and snuffles only a few feet from you, consider putting her in the nursery between feeds at night. If this is the case, make sure to let staff know if you are feeding on demand.

## Routine tests and checks

Throughout your hospital stay, your temperature and pulse will be recorded regularly and your abdomen will be palpated to ensure that the uterus is shrinking as it should. You'll also be asked about your bladder and bowel movements, as constipation is not uncommon at this stage and a laxative may be required. Any stitches and haemhorroids will be observed and treated, and your legs will be checked for any lumps that could indicate clots.

Some time during the first few days, your baby will also undergo the routine check known as the PKU or Guthries test. Her heel is pricked and a few drops of blood are taken and analysed for phenylketonurea, which can cause developmental problems if left untreated. The blood is also tested for cysticfibrosis and galactosaemia and monitors the adequacy of the thyroid gland. Do try to be present when the blood is taken, as your baby would probably appreciate a cuddle afterwards.

## A night out

Some hospitals suggest you have a night out without the baby. This is a good chance to have a quiet evening with your partner, so it's well worth taking up the offer as it may be your last chance for a while. You can be confident that your baby-sitters are about as experienced as they come, and they have the added advantage of being free. If you're breastfeeding, you can either express and leave some milk or go out between feeds. You may need to take the rubber ring to ease the discomfort of stitches.

## PRACTICALITIES

### Birth notices
Most people like to announce the arrival of their baby in one or more of the daily newspapers, even if only to satisfy the proud grandparents. It is worth doing, as a surprising number of people do read the birth notices and it may save a lot of phone calls. It's also a good opportunity to thank the delivery ward staff, if you want to, as they often disappear from your life immediately after the event.

Though you may want a hand in the wording, organising the notice is a good task for your partner, who may be feeling a bit left out of things while you're in hospital. If you're unmarried, or if you commonly use your maiden name, remember to ensure that this gets equal prominence in the notice.

### Thank-yous
If and when flowers and gifts arrive for you and the baby, do keep track of who has sent what. If you have time during your hospital stay, write a few thank-you letters. Before you leave, consider giving the nursing staff flowers or chocolates to thank them for their help.

## BREASTFEEDING: FIRST DAYS

The nursing staff will help you with breastfeeding - suggesting comfortable positions in which to feed, helping the baby to fasten on to the nipple, giving advice about how long each feed should last, and helping you to distinguish hunger cries from those caused by wind or other discomfort. Do, at the same time, use your common sense and do what feels and works best for you and your baby, particularly as you may get conflicting advice from different staff and friends.

If you cannot, or choose not to, breastfeed you may be offered medication to suppress your production of milk. Alternatively, you may be advised to let the milk come in naturally and dry up of its own accord through the lack of stimulation.

Breastfeeding takes both fluid and calories from your body. For as long as you breastfeed, you should eat well and drink as much fluid as your body requests; it is a good policy to have a glass of water or juice within reach every time you sit down to feed.

Try to relax as much as possible before and during feeds, finding a position that is comfortable. If you're concerned whether your baby is getting any milk, be alert for the 'let-down reflex' – this is the contraction of the muscles that propel the milk to the nipple, and is felt by some women as a tingling sensation in the nipples. This reflex may also take place between feeds, when you hear your baby cry, are thinking or talking about your baby, and even during orgasm, so it is advisable to wear nursing pads for protection. Some women are also disconcerted to find breastfeeding sexually stimulating. Don't be concerned if this happens to you, as it is perfectly normal and is caused by the hormone oxytocin.

You may find that your baby becomes a little unsettled two or three days after the birth, about the time when your milk first comes in. This usually means that your milk supply is not yet established; regular feeds will help to rectify this problem.

## Engorgement

On about the third day after the birth, you may wake to find your breasts hot, swollen and tight. Appropriately called 'engorgement', this discomfort is quite normal and is caused by your increased blood supply building up the breast tissue to produce milk. This lasts for a few days at the most – until the volume of milk being produced adjusts to your baby's demands – and you can get some relief by standing under a warm shower or trying light massage. In extreme cases, an analgesic may be recommended.

You may also find that your baby has difficulty latching on to your swollen breast, in which case ask the staff for advice; expressing some milk should help.

## 'Comp' feeds

Some hospitals routinely give babies extra (or complementary) feeds, such as boiled water or a glucose solution, to babies between breastfeeds. Try to ensure that these are not given without your permission: extra food is generally unnecessary and may upset the pattern of demand and supply that underpins breastfeeding.

## Sore nipples

You may find that your nipples become sore, and in extreme cases blister or crack, in the early days of breastfeeding. If problems do occur, ask the nursing staff for advice as blocked mammary ducts can lead to the breast infection known as mastitis.

Methods of treatment for sore nipples tend to go in and out of fashion. Common relief measures include sponging with warm salted water; smearing with a proprietary cream or, even better, with 'hind milk', which has antiseptic and healing properties; or using a ray lamp to promote healing. You should also possibly review your feeding technique: your baby may be sucking for too long, or you may be attaching or detaching her incorrectly.

## DEMAND OR SCHEDULED FEEDING?

Demand feeding means feeding your baby (whether by breast or bottle) whenever she is hungry, which may be anywhere from every two hours to every six hours. The alternative is to offer feeds at set intervals, usually about every four hours.

Like many other aspects of parenting, you are likely to receive conflicting advice about the two approaches, although today demand feeding is generally recommended. There are arguments for and against both systems: with demand feeding, very frequent feeds (at two-hourly intervals or less) may be tiring for the mother. In addition, new mothers·may feel unable to judge whether the baby is crying from hunger or some other cause. Scheduled feeding has the benefit of making your daily life a little more predictable, but does mean that the baby may have to be woken up for feeds.

Some compromise between the two approaches (such as demand feeding at a minimum of three hours) may be advisable for apprehensive or tired mothers.

## DEFLATION

Even while you're still pregnant you'll hear a lot about 'the baby blues' and postnatal depression. The first is common to many new mothers and can occur any time in the first week or so after the birth – it may last a few hours or a few days, or it may bypass you altogether. The baby blues are caused by a combination of hormonal changes, stress, fatigue, and awareness of your new responsibilities. They may take the form of a tendency to dissolve into tears, an overwhelming sense of anticlimax, or simply an inexplicable unhappiness. Don't be too concerned about any irrational or unusual behaviour at this time. Even if there is no apparent reason for the tears, have a good cry or a good talk and wait for them to stop. If you are worried about something in particular, get it off your chest.

Postnatal depression is more severe and a longer-term condition, which occurs in little more than 10 per cent of women. It may manifest itself in overwhelming feelings of inadequacy, isolation, negative feelings about your baby, or guilt. There may be physical symptoms such as pains, diarrhoea or constipation, or loss of appetite. In some women the problem is compounded by a sense of failure and self-blame, which makes them refuse to admit the condition exists or to ask for help. If your baby blues don't go away, or if you feel unable to cope even six months after the birth, talk about it and don't try to be the stalwart supermum. Discuss your feelings with your partner, other mothers, or your doctor or infant-welfare sister. Your partner or family may be able to help by, for example, giving you some free time. You may find that other mothers can provide the sympathy and support you need, or you may need to talk to a counsellor.

## COMMON QUIRKS OF NEWBORN BABIES

There is a lot to learn about your baby and you'll probably find that you while away many hours studying her face and tiny form, noting every flicker of the eyes, every twitch of the nose, and every smiling grimace caused by wind. Handling your baby often will help you gain confidence in your new role.

As you care for your baby in the early days you'll probably notice some or all of the following characteristics. These are common to most newborns, and should not cause you any concern.

### Bowel movements
A newborn baby's stools are generally green and quite sticky for the first few days. This is because they are composed mainly of meconium, or digested mucus from the mucus glands

in the bowel. This will gradually change according to her diet: a breastfed baby's stools are usually soft and yellowish (though sometimes light green owing to wind or an oversupply of milk) and have very little odour. A bottle-fed baby's stools are firmer, brown and smellier.

## Lip blisters
Your baby may develop pale 'sucking' blisters in the first few weeks, which will go away of their own accord and require no treatment.

## Dry skin
Dry or peeling skin, particularly on the hands and feet, is very common in new babies and is unlikely to be eczema. Like the inexplicable spots and blotches to which babies are prone, this condition tends to disappear of its own accord.

## Hiccups, snuffles and twitches
Newborn babies tend to hiccup and snuffle a lot, and often twitch or jerk in their sleep. This can be alarming to new mothers, but as you will soon notice causes your baby no discomfort or distress.

## Weight loss
It is common for babies to lose weight during their first few days out of the womb, as they shed the fluid and nutrients stored up in preparation for the birth. Usually the birth weight is regained, if not surpassed, within a week or so.

## Regurgitating milk

Many babies regurgitate or 'posset' some milk after a feed.
More violent ('projectile') vomiting, while spectacular, is not
uncommon; if it happens regularly, however, you should tell
the nursing staff in case some medication is required.

## Wind

You baby may show signs of discomfort or stomach cramps
from time to time, which usually indicates wind. Although it's
likely that you'll be encouraged to 'burp' your baby after every
feed to expel any wind or gas, don't make a major issue of it
and keep her awake for hours after a feed demanding a result. It
seems that some babies burp and some don't. Burping methods
range from gentle massage to apparently violent thumps on the
back: you will eventually devise a system that suits you and
your baby best.

Regular and severe stomach cramps, where your baby
draws up her legs in apparent agony, may mean colic (see
chapter 8).

# 8 GOING HOME

When the time comes for you to leave hospital, it is likely that you will have mixed feelings – glad to be returning to your own territory, but at least a little doubtful about how you will cope without professional assistance at the end of a buzzer.

The most important goals, as is often the case, will probably be the hardest to achieve – relax, be patient and be flexible. Don't sweep the garden path on your way to the front door; don't take one look in the full-length mirror and head off to the gym; don't criticise your partner if he's slow or clumsy changing that first nappy. Above all, don't assume that your baby will fit into the lifestyle which you had carved for yourselves – there will need to be some adjustments.

## FORMALITIES

### Registering the birth

Within 60 days of the arrival of your baby, you must register the birth with the state registry of births, deaths and marriages. The appropriate form, usually supplied in hospital, must be completed by you and your doctor. If the baby is to take the surname of the father, it may be signed by either partner. If the parents are unmarried, or if the baby is to take a combination surname or the mother's surname, it must be signed by both parents. Once the birth has been registered, an extract of the birth certificate will be forwarded to you (free).

If a baby born after 20 weeks (or weighing more than 400 grams) subsequently dies, both the birth and the death must be registered. In the case of a stillborn baby, or one which lived briefly and was born before 20 weeks or weighed less than 400 grams, no registration is required.

## Family allowance

Hospitals also generally provide application forms for family allowance. This is paid fortnightly, but is subject to a means test for all applicants except those receiving a disability allowance. Ask the hospital or your local infant-welfare sister for more information about special allowances and benefits.

## The local infant-welfare sister

Expect a telephone call or a visit from your local infant-welfare sister within a week or so of your return home. This service provides an invaluable support for new mothers, as the best of these sisters are friendly, helpful and reassuring. Your regular visits to the clinic to weigh the baby, discuss any problems and, if you so desire, make contact with other mothers are well worthwhile.

## Immunisations

Certain immunisations are recommended for your baby from the age of about two months. The first batch comprises a triple antigen injection, usually in the thigh, for whooping cough, diptheria and tetanus, and an oral polio vaccine. Your local council will notify you about these immunisations (which are free) in advance. Doubts have been expressed about the possible side-effects of certain immunisations, but these must be weighed against the dangers posed by the illness itself. If you are concerned, discuss the matter with the sister or your doctor.

## LEARNING TO LIVE WITH A BABY

One of the major shocks for many new mothers is the demands made on their time by a baby. While a newborn may sleep as many as 20 hours a day, this is usually in shortish stretches. In between she needs to be fed and her nappy changed as often as every two to three hours; she also needs cuddles and amusement, and comfort when she cries. Meanwhile there are clothes, bedding and probably nappies to be washed, meals to be cooked, and shopping to be done...

### Getting to know each other

Devote as much time as possible to your baby in the first few weeks, and expect to get little else done while you all adjust to the rhythm and reality of your new life. In essence, make no plans for the first week or so – no shopping expeditions, no social functions, no classes, no big clean-ups, no holidays away. If your partner has managed to take some time off, he should share in handling, bathing and changing the baby.

The best approach is to take life as it comes. At the same time you should gradually try to establish some patterns in your life, if only by bathing the baby at about the same time each day. Don't engage in a frenzied round of outings, tossing her from car capsule to basket and back to capsule, disturbing her 10 times a day, or you'll have very little chance of enjoying a settled baby.

Help her to differentiate between night and day by not extending night feeds with long talks and play: feed, burp and change her, and encourage her to go back to sleep. If you have trouble settling her again after a feed, call on your partner to take the second shift.

Above all, observe and listen to your baby. Take note of her sleeping and wakeful times, and also of her feeds. Observe the position she prefers to sleep in, and whether she likes being swaddled or struggles to free herself.

Keep her close by you in the early days. If you're working around the house or garden, or just relaxing, keep her bassinet or pram nearby. Don't feel you have to tiptoe about when she is asleep.


## Household chores

As you'll have your hands fairly full just meeting your baby's basic needs, you may find that other domestic chores lag behind. Don't be too concerned, even if you're traditionally efficient in this area, as the odd bit of dust won't hurt. You may need to rethink your priorities in the short term.

If the processing of nappies is proving to be a problem, again consider a nappy-wash service or at least the partial use of disposables.

While washing can't be avoided, and in fact may keep you or your partner far busier than you could have expected, ironing is not essential. In the first few weeks, try to avoid wearing items which need to be ironed and consider which of your baby's things really require it. Your partner can do his own ironing, if it's essential.

## Pets

If you have pets, there is no need to banish them to the garden. Health experts say that our pets are in more danger of catching diseases from us than we are from them. Make sure cats and dogs are wormed regularly, however, and that hands are washed between touching them and baby. Be aware that some cats are notorious for wanting to curl up close to the head. Be observant for any signs of jealousy, though this is less likely to occur if pets are at least allowed to sniff the baby and if you show you still love them.

## WHAT ABOUT YOU?

It is unlikely that you'll regain your old vitality for several weeks, and possibly months. Your hormones and your body are still readjusting, and stitches may still be healing. While your dependent baby tends to come first, make sure that you at least come second.

Don't make yourself indispensable and don't be over-protective with your baby. Encourage your partner to be an active participant rather than just a helper, and accept assistance from friends or family if and when it's offered.

A lack of sleep is probably the most debilitating problem for new mothers. Particularly if you're breastfeeding or are recovering from a difficult birth, try to get some rest during the day. Put your feet up as often as possible if you can't manage a nap: the more rest you get, the better you'll be able to care for your baby and cope with the demands on you.

You may find that friends, family and even acquaintances are eager to visit. If you feel up to it, by all means let them come but don't feel that you have to live up to your old standards of hospitality. If, on the other hand, you feel too tired or simply too flustered to entertain, tactfully tell them so.

## Guilt, panic and the whole damn thing

Be prepared for some unpredictable emotions in the early weeks, as your hormones readjust and tiredness takes its toll.

A fragmented day can be frustrating, particularly if you've achieved nothing tangible at the end of it. Expect to have mixed and confusing feelings in the early weeks – a sense of over-whelming love for your baby may be followed rapidly by equally overwhelming misgivings about your new responsibilities or even resentment at the intrusion on your old way of life.

You'll undoubtedly do a lot of worrying about your baby. Why is she crying this time? Is she getting enough (or too much) to drink? Should she lie on her back or her front? Is her room too hot (or too cold)? Worrying is normal, but try not to overdo it and do remember that babies are remarkably resilient.

You may also have some less familiar feelings. Frustration, irritability, guilt and even boredom are common, and can be relieved by some time off – either with your partner or by yourself if he is available to babysit, even for an hour or two. If you are constantly depressed or really feel you can't cope, discuss your concerns with your partner, your infant-welfare sister or your doctor.

## YOU AND YOUR PARTNER

As a dependent baby tends to become a mother's first priority, your relationship with your partner will inevitably change. Your roles will alter, and the quality and quantity of your time together will alter. Matters may be further complicated by your emotional state: you may feel isolated, lacking in self-esteem, resentful, and low in libido.

Communication is perhaps even more important now than it was during pregnancy, when there were still just two of you. Try to set aside some time to talk to each other and don't exclude your partner from, or because of, your relationship with your baby. Tell him of your concerns, and take time to listen to his. It is also important for you to find time to be, or go out, alone with your partner. Time together outside the home is often much more valuable and relaxing than time together while baby is asleep. Don't feel guilty about escaping.

## Sex

Resume sex whenever you and your partner feel physically and mentally comfortable with the idea, unless you have received other advice from your doctor. It may take a couple of months for you to summon up the energy, let alone find a suitable time.

You may feel tense or apprehensive the first time, especially if you had an episiotomy or caesarian, so proceed with caution as there is no value in painful sex. An episiotomy scar may be tender six to eight weeks after the birth.

In the early postnatal days, as your hormone levels are returning to normal and if you're breastfeeding, your vagina may need extra lubrication. For comfort's sake you may need to experiment with different positions, and tender breasts may also need to be handled with extra delicacy. If you're breastfeeding you may find that the let-down reflex is triggered by orgasm. If this bothers you or your partner, push down firmly on your nipples when you feel the response. If any problems such as vaginal dryness persist, see your doctor.

Above all, the time for sex may need some revision. You may feel too tired at the end of a long day, so consider the morning instead.

## Contraception

The question of contraception is often on the top of the list when you return to your doctor for your six-week check.

Breastfeeding is not a reliable means of contraception. Although research suggests that 80 per cent of women who breastfeed will not be fertile until after their first period (it rarely occurs before 20 weeks), it has been known for women to conceive again three weeks after the birth.

The best early options are a condom, spermicide or diaphragm, natural contraception (such as the Billings, temperature and rhythm methods once you're ovulating again), or the minipill (progesterone only). The standard pill disrupts your milk flow and can have hormonal effects on the baby.

## FEEDING: SOME TIPS

Once you're at home, the practices you learned in hospital may desert you or you may find that you establish new systems that suit you and your baby better. Whatever the case, many new mothers find that feeding their newborn – whether by breast or by bottle – is not as simple as they expected. If you do have problems, discuss them with your infant-welfare sister. The nursery staff at your hospital may also be willing to give you some 'aftercare' advice.

### Breastfeeding

Bear in mind that it may take up to six weeks for your milk supply to become properly established. If your baby is unsettled or not putting on the expected amount of weight, you may need to offer more frequent feeds to build up your supply.

Always be as comfortable as possible before and during a feed, and have a glass of water or juice beside you. If it makes you feel more relaxed, take the phone off the hook and put a 'Please don't disturb' sign on your front door.

If you have trouble remembering which breast to offer first, wear a safety pin on your bra as a reminder.

If you are having problems breastfeeding, contact the Nursing Mothers' Association in your area. Many branches have a 24-hour telephone counselling service.

## ... and escaping

Breastfeeding need not prevent you working or just getting out for a day or night, as you can express and store milk on a regular basis. If you were not shown how to express in hospital, ask a friend or your infant-welfare sister to show you how.

Expressing milk can be difficult at first, with quite a bit of effort required for little reward, but it does give you some freedom with the confidence that your baby is still receiving your milk. It can also make you more comfortable if your breasts are overfull. Breast milk will keep for about 48 hours in a refrigerator, for about two weeks in the fridge freezer, and considerably longer in a freestanding freezer. The frozen milk should be thawed in the fridge and used within 12 hours.

If you're at work and missing three feeds, express at about the baby's feeding-time and store the milk to take home for the next day.

Some women don't enjoy expressing milk; if you don't it doesn't mean that you need be completely hamstrung, as an occasional bottle of formula is unlikely to have dire effects on either your baby or your milk supply.

## Bottle-feeding

When preparing formula, always follow the manufacturer's instructions exactly. Don't worry about any drops of sterilising solution that cling to the bottle and teat: it may not taste appealing, but is scarcely noticeable when diluted with formula and certainly will not harm your baby. As with breastfeeding, make yourself and your baby comfortable before offering the bottle. You may need to experiment with different teats before you find one that suits your baby.

Bear in mind that a few babies are allergic to standard formulas. If she is particularly unsettled, this is one possible explanation. Ask your infant-welfare sister for advice.

Show your partner how to do prepare the formula and give your baby a bottle, and encourage him to feed her as often as possible.

## CRYING BABIES

Babies generally cry much more than you expect. While you may learn to recognise hunger cries quite early on, it's less easy to distinguish causes such as pain, sadness, boredom, loneliness or frustration. While it may be little comfort when it happens, the fact is that many babies have unsettled days during their first weeks at home.

The first thing to remember is that you won't spoil your baby by going to her when she cries – this is, after all, the only means of communication she has.  As a first step, offer her a feed, burp her in case of residual wind, change her nappy, check that she is not too hot or too cold (feeling inside the clothing at her neck), give her a cuddle or a dummy, and rock her and sing.

The second line of defence is to put her in a pram or sling and go for a walk, or take her for a drive, as movement and fresh air will often put a baby to sleep. Other possible remedies include a weak brew of herbal tea (such as peppermint or camomile), gentle massage, or a warm bath.

## ... and crying mothers

If such measures fail and your baby seems inconsolable, it can be very distressing. Prolonged crying tends to generate anxiety and feelings of inadequacy or failure in a mother, which can be made worse if you're very tired. If all else fails and you're feeling over-wrought, get yourself out of earshot – if only for five minutes – and if possible hand her over to your partner or a friend. If no help is at hand, ring your infant-welfare sister for advice.

## Colic

If your baby cries persistently and no relief measures have any effect, she may have colic – a broad term for various abdominal cramps. Typical symptoms include spasms of pain during which the baby draws up her legs, a desperate sucking of the fingers or fists, and sharp distinctive cries. It occurs most commonly in the evening or at night, and may continue in bouts for several hours.

Colic is extremely upsetting for parents, as they are forced to watch their baby in apparent agony. The condition may last for up to three months, which seems like a lifetime of nights pacing the floor with your inconsolable baby. While there is no cure for colic, there are a number of measures which may bring temporary relief:

- raise the head of her bassinet to help expel any painful wind
- place a warm (covered) hot-water bottle against her abdomen
- offer a dummy, as sucking seems to help (but drinking seems to make it worse)
- try gentle massage, particularly of the abdominal area, or bicycle her legs back and forth
- put her in a deep warm bath
- rock her relatively vigorously, in your arms or in her pram-stroller

If colic persists, seek help from your infant-welfare sister or doctor.

## SHAPING UP

Your pre-pregnancy wardrobe may be both an irritation and an incentive in early postnatal days. Returning to your old self is a matter not merely of shedding a few excess kilos, but of encouraging the stretched and strained parts back into the shape they were in before the birth.

The answer, of course, is a sensible diet. Breastfeeding coupled with a mother's fairly active lifestyle could well see your pre-pregnancy weight regained effortlessly. Alternatively, you may have to monitor your intake of food and liquids. In general you should follow the same dietary guidelines suggested during your pregnancy (see chapter 2). Beware of constant snacking, particularly if this became a habit during pregnancy to alleviate nausea or heartburn. Beware also of sweet drinks, particularly if you are drinking a lot more because you're breastfeeding.

## Exercise

Exercise is all-important – not toe-tapping aerobics, but the more sedate kind designed specifically to tone your body. You may opt for the stimulus and social contact of postnatal exercise classes, or you may prefer to regain your shape in the privacy of your own home. Whatever the case, you should exercise for 10 to 15 minutes every day, preferably in the morning before you become too tired.

## THE SIX-WEEK CHECK

This checkup with your doctor is to ensure that your body is returning to normal and that you are in good mental and physical health. (Your doctor may or may not ask to see your baby.) This is also your chance to ask questions about the birth, about your recovery, and about suitable forms of contraception.

The extent of the examination will depend upon whether the pregnancy and the birth were normal. The doctor may palpate your abdomen and examine your cervix to determine if the uterus has returned to normal. She may also take a cervical smear, depending on when the last one was done.

## GETTING OUT AND ABOUT

Once the dust has settled, getting out and about again – both with and without your baby – should be a priority. Babies are very portable for the first few months and can be taken just about anywhere, from supermarkets to restaurants. The main requirements are a clean place to change her and, if she is bottle-fed, ensuring her bottle is kept cold and can be warmed when she needs it.

### The baby bag

Make sure that the baby bag has everything you think you're going to need. Even if you're only going out for an hour, put in two nappies instead of one, a clean outfit, and so on. It should also contain a spare rug, and plenty of tissues or cotton balls.

It is sensible to keep the bag permanently packed, refilling it as soon as you get home so that you can grab it and depart at a moment's notice.

### Babysitters

Enthusiastic family members obviously make the best baby-sitters – if they are available. If they're not, the best way to find baby-sitters is to inquire: ask your local infant-welfare sister, ask neighbours, ask friends in similar situations. If these avenues are fruitless, check the child-care section of your local paper and consider a baby-sitting agency or nanny service.

You should interview any potential babysitter, even if she comes recommended. For your own sake, it's important that you have total confidence in her and feel that she is doing it because she likes babies rather than simply for the money. If possible, try to get someone who lives nearby or at least has reliable transport, as you may not feel like driving her home across three suburbs at the end of a long day or evening out.

## Classes and groups

If you're feeling isolated, consider joining a local postnatal exercise class. This gives you the dual benefit of helping you regain your former shape while giving you some social contact. Many organisers encourage you to bring your baby, and some have creche facilities. Ask your infant-welfare sister about groups or clubs in your area.

There are also numerous classes for and about babies – on baby massage, baby gyms or swims, and even music appreciation. If you find the idea appealing it's worth enrolling, but rest assured that you won't be depriving your baby of stimulus if you are either unable or unwilling to join.

When your baby is a little older, and if you're not working, consider joining (or even organising) a playgroup. These can be as formal or as informal as you wish, and have proved invaluable contact for many housebound mothers – even those who don't particularly relish group activities. However humble, playgroups can be fun as well as educational and stimulating.

## CHILD CARE

You may also be in the market for regular child care, if only for one morning a week. The options include child-care centres, family day care (where your baby is looked after in the home of an approved 'carer') or someone who comes into your own home.

If you haven't done so already, consider your needs and preferences: if you're breastfeeding, for example, having your baby looked after at home is particularly convenient. Talk to any friends who have used different forms of child care, and ask them about the pros and cons. If you opt for a child-care centre, contact those in your area and visit them before you make any commitment as it's important that you feel happy with both the facilities and the atmosphere. The same applies to family day care.

If you choose to employ someone in your home, it may be a nanny or a mothercraft nurse. While nannies are generally much cheaper, many are young and inexperienced; a mother-craft nurse, on the other hand, has tertiary training and usually several years of experience. Ask your friends or local infant-welfare sister for a recommendation, and also inquire about typical hourly rates. Alternatively, check the ads – or put your own – in your local paper. Again, whatever your decision be rigorous in your selection process, particularly as this person will be spending a lot of time in your house.

Be prepared for the fact that finding good child care is time-consuming. Regular child care is often costly, too, although government centres offer reduced fees for low-income earners. Do remember, however, that as yet child care is not tax-deductible.

Whichever form of child care you choose, allow a settling-in period for all of you, as you are likely to suffer from both guilt and separation anxiety the first few times you leave your baby. If this is the case, just grit your teeth and get out: babies have a remarkable ability to stop crying the minute you're out of sight.

# 9 SOME TIPS FOR FATHERS

Once your partner announces she's pregnant, you've got only a few months to become accustomed – and above all committed – to a challenging new chapter in your life.

The role of fathers has changed dramatically in the last 20 years or so. For centuries they were principally the head of the household and usually the sole breadwinner. As far as being a parent was concerned, fathers – as was hoped of their children – were most commonly seen and not heard, except perhaps when some disciplinary action was required. Today things are very different: your partner and even your peers now have quite definite expectations about the part you can play in pregnancy, in the birth itself, and in the everyday care of your child.

Pregnancy and parenthood bring many and often unexpected rewards, not least of which is a remarkable new love in your life. They also bring nights of interrupted sleep, a loss of spontaneity in your social life, and new expenses. As far as your relationship is concerned, it means putting up with the idiosyncrasies of a pregnant partner, with reduced sex for weeks or even months, and with taking what may appear to be a back seat in your partner's life once the baby is born. Your priorities about work and leisure will probably change, and you may at times feel weighed down by your new responsibilities. At the same time, as any father will tell you, the more involved you become with your partner and your baby during this time, the more fulfilling and enjoyable the experience will be.

## WHAT TO EXPECT IN THE COMING MONTHS

Pregnancy, however burdensome, is perhaps easier for a woman to come to terms with than is the case for a man. She is part of it, while you are in many ways merely a spectator.

To make life easier for both of you, it is important to have some idea of what to expect. As well as the the more predictable changes in your partner's shape, you should be prepared for a number of other physical and emotional developments. Most of these are produced by the onslaught of specialised hormones in her body throughout the pregnancy. Other changes may be caused by simple reactions such as fear (of the pain of childbirth, or of her future life as a mother), or the loss of confidence in her appearance as she becomes more and more bulky.

Among the most common characteristics of pregnancy are mood swings, tiredness and forgetfulness. It is difficult to generalise, as pregnancy affects every woman differently: a placid woman may become emotional and weepy, while a volatile one may become unrecognisably serene. You should be prepared, however, for the fact that she will become tired as her body works overtime to support the developing baby, and that she will undergo – at least occasionally – baffling emotional lows.

# WHAT YOU CAN DO

Try to organise some leave around the time the baby is due, keeping the dates a bit flexible in case she is early or late. It's generally agreed, even by the most unwilling fathers, that the more time and affection you devote to your baby in the early months, the more you'll get out of the relationship the long term.

In pregnancy, forewarned is definitely forearmed. It is worth reading the books on pregnancy and parenthood that are now likely to be on the bookshelf. It is also important to remember that any unusual traits are temporary only, and are to a large extent beyond your partner's control.

## Physical changes

If you find her changing shape worrisome or even offputting, rest assured that this too is temporary. Try to reassure her that she's still attractive. Encourage her in sensible eating and drinking habits, but don't push too hard – she may feel she needs some compensation. If she's tired, encourage her to rest and try to carry some of the burden of household chores.

## Communication

Talk to your partner, telling her of any concerns or fears you may have and listening to hers. Try to be patient in the face of temperamental displays.

## Sharing the pregnancy

There are many ways in which you can take part in the pregnancy. If she is to have an ultrasound scan, it's well worth attending: it gives you a remarkable image of the foetus, which is often the first real evidence a father has of his baby's existence. If you are planning to attend the birth, it is also worthwhile attending the antenatal classes with your partner, as they offer useful information about what you can expect during pregnancy and the birth itself, and how you can help. Also talk to any of your friends who have been through the experience already, as this will give you a realistic appraisal from the male point of view.

## ABOUT THE BIRTH

It is now common for fathers to attend the birth of their child. Discuss with your partner whether you want to be present, and whether she wants you there. Even if your initial response to the idea is negative, do give it serious consideration as many fathers see this as the most moving experience of their lives. On the other hand, don't feel compelled to attend the birth just because it's the done thing, as some men do find it harrowing.

If you choose to be at the birth, discuss with your partner the sort of birth she wants, so that if necessary you can advise the doctor about her wishes in matters such as pain relief. Be prepared to be flexible, however, as the best-laid plans may alter if there are unforeseen complications. Childbirth is not the time to assert your dominance, over either your partner or the staff in attendance.

Your presence will undoubtedly provide moral support for your partner during labour and the birth. There are also many ways in which you can play an active part, from massage during the early stages to physical support if she chooses to kneel or squat for the delivery. As the nursing staff may be needed elsewhere from time to time, you may also be able to monitor the progress of labour on their behalf.

## And afterwards

Don't forget to have a bottle of champagne at the ready for after the birth. A camera or video for some early photos is also recommended, but if you'd like to film the birth itself make sure your partner is agreeable as this may not be the most flattering light in which to be immortalised on film.

Spend as much time as possible at the hospital, as it's an important time to get to know your baby and to give your partner support and reassurance. It's quite likely that you'll feel a bit left out at this time, but you can keep involved by getting the house in order, organising the birth notice, or notifying distant friends or family. As the baby will probably be showered with gifts, consider buying one for your partner too.

## BACK AT HOME

From the day mother and baby return home from hospital, your life will no longer be the same. The first weeks with a new baby can be very demanding. Babies need to be fed and their nappies changed up to a dozen times a day; they generate remarkable amounts of washing and ironing relative to their size; they need a lot of love and affection; and they seem to cry a lot, often for no apparent reason. Meanwhile, you and your partner also need food, clean clothes, some time to relax, and – above all – some sleep.

Even if the birth was easy, your partner is likely to be very tired for some time after she returns home. As her hormones adjust she may be prone to tearfulness, confused emotions, or a loss of self-confidence. She may also be apprehensive about her new role, about her inevitably changed relationship with you, and about her shape.

## What you can do

In short, you will probably need great patience as all three of you go through a potentially difficult settling-in period. There will also be the added strains that tiredness can bring. If you can't organise time off work, try to make sure that you keep your weekends free so that you share both the chores and the cuddles.

If the baby is being breastfed you can't take over that particular job, but you can play a part by making sure that your partner is relaxed. You can certainly share other aspects of everyday care, from burping and bathing the baby to nappy-changing.

Do your share of the houshold tasks too, whether by cooking meals, doing the shopping, or washing clothes and nappies. If possible, give your partner some time off without the baby and try to make sure that you both have some time together. Be patient about resuming sex.

# The arsenic hour

One of the most difficult times of the day for new parents seems to be about 5–6 p.m., often called the 'arsenic hour'. If you work a 9–5 day, you'll probably arrive home at exactly this time. Your partner is likely to be frazzled, your baby is probably due for a feed, and there's no sign of dinner being prepared. While it's reasonable for you to hope for some attention and a little nurturing, it is likely to be in short supply. Your partner may be despondent at having achieved little other than looking after the baby, and irritated by your offers of news from the outside world. Again, be patient: hold off unburdening your tales of the day's successes or frustrations, and instead take the baby for a cuddle and nappy-change.

# Postnatal depression

Many women are prone to a period of confusion and tear-fulness in the early days after giving birth. In a small number of cases, this can develop into postnatal depression, a persistent and serious psychological condition which requires treatment or counselling. The symptoms of postnatal depression may be physical (pains, or loss of appetite) or emotional (loss of self-confidence, excessive feelings of guilt or isolation, inability to cope, or confused feelings towards her baby). If you are concerned that your partner may be suffering from postnatal depression, encourage her to discuss her feelings with the local infant-welfare sister or with her doctor.